MEDIA MANUALS

Scriptwriting for Animation

MEDIA MANUALS

Scriptwriting for Animation

Stan
Hayward

A Focal Press Book

Communication Arts Books
HASTINGS HOUSE, PUBLISHERS
New York, NY 10016

ISBN 8038-6741-7
Library of Congress
Catalog Card Number: 77-80649

Printed and Bound in England by A. Wheaton & Co. Exeter

ontents

INTRODUCTION

'Philosophy is the science of possible worlds (Bertrand Russell) 'Animation is the art of possible worlds' . . . (Anonymous . . . though it might have been me). It is certain though that the only real thing in animation is the *idea*. Images are shot frame by frame, so are never actually moving; nor do any of the characters, objects, or effects have a parallel in real life other than by analogy. Yet in spite of bending the laws of space, time and reason to the limits of imagination, animated films tend to come over larger than life. This is because, above all other film techniques, animation allows concepts to be isolated, analysed, reinforced, and presented in a direct form that is immediate and obvious.

Defining concepts, and putting them into a form that is cinematically workable is the *craft* of scriptwriting. I use the word 'craft' rather than 'art', because film making is a technical medium, and however talented and inspired one might be as a writer, the 'phrase that comes trippingly off the tongue' will be totally wasted unless there are clear cut instructions on where the camera should be at the time.

Animation is the most technical of mediums. Every dot, line, colour and movement has to be consciously put down with a given end in view. An idea that is fuzzy in the script stage, will certainly be fuzzy on the screen. nothing happens by chance other than bad accidents. Nor do bright ideas that come as afterthoughts have much chance of inclusion in a film once the production has started. The bulk of the creative work - be it script, design, dialogue or music, is conceived and finalised before the first frame is animated.

Animation scriptwriters, do not exist in the sense that film and television scriptwriters do — as writers involved in full time writing. Most animated films are short in script but long in production, so the chances are that the 'animation scriptwriter' will be someone who works in animation, and has to produce a script, or someone who writes, teaches or produces in some other medium and has need of animation. The aim of the book is to compliment the skills of those who need to write for animation. It is not meant to teach animation other than where the techniques have a direct bearing on the preparation of a script; nor is it meant to teach the art of creative writing other than to suggest creative use of the medium. But, given that the reader has an idea he feels worthwhile, he will certainly be able to produce a storyboard that is ready for production having used this book as a guide and source of reference.

The Storyboard

The scriptwriter's job is to take an idea and make it into a working plan of a film ready to go into production. This plan is called a storyboard and is arrived at in several stages.

Idea
The idea, or basic concept of the film can be summed up by its title, or a brief description: 'The Story of the Motor Car!' 'The Adventures of Willie the Bear!' or, 'Snow White and the Seven Dwarfs. An animated musical based upon the story.'

Ideas fall into two broad categories: those derived from an existing source such as a book; and those originated for the medium of animated film.

Outline
Even derived ideas will need to be restructured and given an outline. The key points, beginning/middle/end are defined, and the situations, styling and staging are developed around these. The 'fuzzy' parts that link the key points are left to be resolved at a later stage when characters and key situations have been defined. Rough sketches are done at this stage.

Treatment
The key points are linked by a storyline. The rough sketches are developed, action and dialogue are separated (see Writing Formats page 16) and the creative and production problems are given due consideration. It is at this point that story weaknesses become evident. These can sometimes be strengthened by design, effects, or soundtrack, which are then indicated in the script.

Storyboard
The treatment is visualised in 'comic strip' form, showing camera shots, effects, transitions, titles and credits. Spaces should be left for live action shots where these are to be included.

This is a 'rough storyboard' for the studio, but often it is necessary for the studio to produce a final 'presentation storyboard' for the client. This is in full colour and mounted on cardboard backing. It clearly indicates what the film will look like, and gives all the details on timing and effects that take place.

The scriptwriter's job should be finished at this stage, but even the most carefully checked storyboard can have hidden traps, and may require a later rewrite. Anticipating these traps is also part of his job.

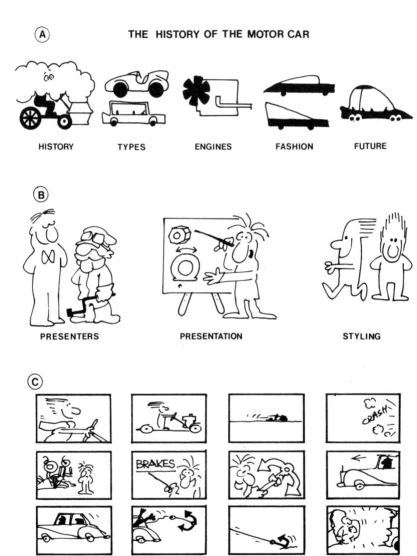

STORYBOARD DEVELOPMENT

A. Outline. B. Treatment. C. Rough Storyboard.

Drawing Up A Storyboard

It is the scriptwriter's job to produce a visual interpretation of his script. It need only be drawn, or designed in an elementary way, but it does have to convey the essential information on scale, positions, relationships between images, direction of movement, and angles of view.

Formula figures
Simple formulae figures can be adapted for any situation by the addition of props and words to indicate what is happening (see Props page 74). Remember that the eyes, mouth, and hands are the main features to concentrate on to convey meaning and show action.

Stencils and drawing aids
Plastic stencils are made for most technical requirements, with many special stencils for subjects like chemistry, architecture, and engineering. Apart from these, with a little ingenuity you can convert knives and forks, wire and plastic into stencils by tracing around and bending, cutting and combining shapes.

Other ready-made shapes come in the form of 'instant' lettering which includes colours, textures, and figures in the range. These can be added to existing artwork or photos to build up images.

Copying machines
Reference books used for the script may contain suitable illustrations for the storyboard. By running off several copies of the same diagram and painting out the parts not needed, or adding extra artwork, a sequence can be shown without having to repeat the original artwork. Existing copyrights should be observed.

Magazines
Always keep well illustrated magazines, brochures, advertising literature, etc. These provide a wealth of material to cut out, trace off, and paste up. Fit these under broad headings such as Buildings, People, Animals, Machinery, Landscapes, etc. These pictures will indicate 'the sort of thing' you want, and become a placeholder until the final storyboard is drawn up.

Reference books
There are a number of artist's reference books available that simplify and give a range of drawings on a particular subject. These can be easily copied and traced over.

Practise using existing visual material where this is readily available, and always keep pictures, diagrams, charts, etc, of anything that you have a feeling might be useful.

DRAWING AIDS

Formula figures; using a basic shape for a range of characters. B. Stencils and
printed figures. C. Instant lettering and magazine cutouts. D. Copying machine.

Timing . . . The Key to Animation

Timing operates on three levels:
1. The gestures and movements of the individual character or objec
2. The pace of the action within the scene.
3. The rhythm of the scenes as a sequence.

Movement and gestures

Animation is a dialogue of action and reaction, with all movements e
aggerated. This exaggeration is emphasised by effects, e.g. Fast-ru
ning rabbit skids and screeches to a stop with smoke coming from h
heels.

Gestures define the character as strong, weak, nervous, etc, an
these gestures have to be timed to emphasise the spoken word an
accentuate the action. There has to be a 'balance' of gestures betwee
the characters so that body movements communicate the situatio
There should also be 'sympathy' movements with the surrounding o
jects and characters so that the screen does not become static.

Pace

Pace is the rate at which the story unfolds. It varies with the conte
of the scene. There should be a balance between the active an
passive scenes so that the audience does not get bored, or is unable
follow what is going on. A guide to this is to separate the 'heavy' pa
of the message that needs some thought, from the 'light' parts whi
may be used as linking sequences.

Watch films and count the number of cuts and transitions in
scene. This is how live-action films create pace. Animation achieve
the same end by increasing or decreasing the amount of informatio
on the screen.

Rhythm

Rhythm is how the scenes are put together so that the heavy and lig
scenes are spaced to give a sense of tension and relaxation. The fil
as a whole should gather pace — in effect, a speed up in the rhythm
as the information establishes itself and more can be put into ea
scene.

MOVEMENT RHYTHM AND PACE

A. Gesture of a character in one part of the screen. B. Movement of a character across the screen. C. As information increases, so does the action and reaction. D. Graph showing rhythm of scenes plotted against the pace of action within the scenes.

15

Writing Formats

Writing for *content* means stating the sequence of ideas as a basic structure for the film. These ideas should not be too descriptive otherwise they tend to be taken for the actual script. Writing for *style* means putting down clear cut instructions on what is happening – and when. Here is a fifteen-sec. TV commercial roughed out for content, then written down as a shooting script.

An aerosol can of Moonshine furniture polish animates to look like a rocket ship. A housewife dressed like an astronaut gets in and shoots around the room spraying the furniture so that it sparkles.

It is common practice to use capital letters for instructions and visuals, but normal letters for dialogue.

VISUAL	SOUND
C.U. OF MOONSHINE AEROSOL CAN ON TABLE AS ESTABLISHING SHOT.	
CUT BACK. IT ANIMATES TO LOOK LIKE ROCKET SHIP BUT RETAINS LOGO.	
ASTRONAUT COMES ON AND GETS INTO THE ROCKET SHIP WHICH THEN TAKES OFF.	FOOTSTEPS TAKE-OFF SOUNDS
ROCKET SHOOTS AROUND ROOM SPRAYING THE WOODEN FURNITURE. IT SPARKLES LIKE STARS.	HARP SOUNDS.
ROCKET RETURNS AND LANDS ON TABLE. AN ASTRONAUT GETS OUT. ROCKET ANIMATES BACK TO AEROSOL CAN.	
ASTRONAUT TAKES OFF VISOR. WE SEE IT IS A HOUSEWIFE. SHE GESTURES TO THE CAN.	"Moonshine . . . the space age furniture polish that will put stars in your eyes next time you do the housework."
LOGO ON CAN SPARKLES. HOLD ON LOGO FOR THREE SECONDS.	

There should be enough information in this script to produce a storyboard with the aid of the photos or designs of the pack.

SCRIPT FORMAT

As visualised from the written script this is the rough storyboard. A. C.U. of can. Zoom back to show it as a rocket ship. B. Astronaut walks on, track in to door. C. Rocket takes off. D. Cut to room. The can sprays the furniture which sparkles. E. Cut to wider shot to show sparkling furniture. F. Cut to can landing. G. Astronaut comes out, walks up to camera, removes helmet. H. Seen to be housewife. She says: 'Moonshine, the space age polish that puts stars in *your* eyes every time you do the housework.'

17

Keeping it Simple

Simple viewing is hard writing. The greatest compliment a scriptwriter can get is for someone to think that the message is 'obvious' – and so it should be, once written. One of the problems facing the writer is that having worked on a script for some time, many of the difficult parts begin to seem obvious when, in fact, they are not. These parts may become skimped instead of receiving the full coverage they need.

Simplifying starts with choosing the right words – the shortest and the commonest words that suit the purpose. If you are writing about rockets you might put 'The trajectory of the missile through the atmosphere' which could be simplified to: 'the curve of the rocket through the air'. The latter has a better rhythm and stronger visual connotations.

A moving image in competition with words will always attract the most attention, so try not to put key words over a strong moving image. These words should come before, or after the movement to anticipate or sum up the visual statement. Think of movements as being contained within basic shapes: circles, squares, triangles, these should be in the centre of the picture area, otherwise the eye 'follows through' and goes out of the screen. The shapes themselves should be simple, and uncluttered with detail. They should preferably move forward and back in the screen rather than across it.

Abstracting

Sometimes a difficult idea has to be put across and there is, or seems to be, no easy way to do this in the time available. The choice appears to be between putting the idea in and hoping it is understood, or extending it at the expense of some other idea. One approach is to abstract the difficult idea and treat it as though it were the basis of the film, and then to write the film around it. Seen in this context the related ideas are then given other priorities and can be reconsidered in terms of their contribution to the whole.

Never try to 'wedge' an idea into the script to make a point clear. If you have to add amendments then the idea has not been stated clearly enough in the first place. Go back to the concept stage and sum up the idea again in one sentence, then see in how many ways it can be developed – otherwise the flow of ideas will be broken and the storyline may appear contrived.

Very few animated films run for more than a few minutes (the bulk of the exceptions being in entertainment). In those few minutes you will be luckly if you can put over three ideas in a memorable way. Aim at this number. Let someone *not* working on the script read it, and then ask them to sum up the film. If they pick up the three basic ideas then the script is doing its job.

Voice:	Directions:
Compression	very slow movement.

Ignition.	piston moves down as spark ignites.

Exhaust.	piston expels gasses.

Induction.	New gas sucked in. Completes cycle. Accelerate cycle; add sound effects remove voice.

MATCHING TRACK TO VISUAL

State what is happening before it happens to prepare the viewer. Don't put key words over key movements. Establish ideas at each stage first, then put them together. Make each idea clear before moving onto the next one.

Never assume it will be all right on the day.

Nothing Happens by Chance

Except accidents. It is not the writer's job to decide on how every dot, line, colour, and movement in the film is to be done. But *someone* has to, and it is the writer's job to see that the original intentions of the script are adhered to.

A typical problem is a character that 'gets away' from the script, particularly in TV commercials where a funny character comes out and does his bit and goes off. Everyone laughs and thinks it is a great bit of animation, but no one can remember what was being advertised!

This problem can be forced on the writer by a sponsor insisting that a well-established character be used, or by the creation of a character that will be automatically identified with other established animated figures.

Interpretation

Situations can also get out of hand and move off in directions inconsistent with the storyline. For example, take a line in the script that says:

'A cat comes into a bar and orders a drink. He swills it down and is knocked out by it'.

This might be interpreted by the animator in several ways.

1. Cat pours drink down his throat. His toes glow and the colour rises like a thermometer and hits his head and explodes.

2. Cat swigs drink in one shot. His eyes rattle together, then he goes stiff and keels over like a felled tree.

3. Takes drink casually, then a silly smile comes over his face as he collapses over a bar stool like a wet rag, then slides off on to the floor and flattens out like a bear rug.

4. Cat casually takes drink, then lights a cigarette. The cigarette burns down like a fuse, the cat's toes start to smoke and then he rumbles and shoots off like a rocket into space.

Each interpretation is suitable as an analogy for being hit by a drink, but each one would leave a different situation to be resolved. It is the accumulation of such minor events that over the period of the film can give it a direction and feeling quite different from that intended.

Rationale

The rationale is a term that covers the brief description of why you are approaching the story in such a way, and what you intend it to achieve. It is worthwhile writing one out before you start the script, or if you find the story is slipping away from you.

INTERPRETING THE SCRIPT

A. In commercials keep the product dominant. (1) Wrong, character dominates product. (2) Better, character presents product.

B. Interpretations of a cat taking a drink. Each has to be resolved differently.

21

Copyright

The writer is responsible for checking that the material, references, photos, diagrams, soundtracks, quotations, etc., to be used in the film are available.

Often a book will inspire a film — in several different people at the same time. Even using a book as only the *basis* for a film can result in the embarrassment of finding another production covering much the same ground in the same way.

If you do wish to use the book as the basis for a script then check with *both* publisher and author. The copyright between them may be open to various interpretations. I have known a producer to pay for a film title (which is not copyright) and an author to give permission for his work to be used when the publisher owned the copyright, and later refused permission!

It has even been known for the 'walk cycle' of an animated character to be copyright; and 'guest' appearances of well-known animated figures in films without permission can cause problems. It is also a common mistake with students to use a record of a popular song to back their work, only later to find that the film could not be distributed until the royalties were paid.

Guides on copyright can be obtained in the UK from the Performing Rights Society, the *Writers and Artists Yearbook*, and public libraries.

Having stated the above as a warning, from the storyboard point of view anything that is not to be shown publicly is unlikely to cause an infringement. Nor is it likely that individual photos, diagrams or snatches of tunes are likely to cause much bother if they are not exploited blatantly in a film. It is common practice to use photo montage as an animation technique.

The same rules apply to the writer in anything created. If you define a character, or a set of them, and these become the basis for the film, it is worth checking with the film unions or guilds whether or not you retain the copyright on them, especially if they may later be exploited as toys, T-shirts, or in another medium.

CREATOR OF CHARACTER

OWNER OF COPYRIGHT

CHECK OWNERSHIP FIRST

If you create a character, remember you can copyright it and still sell the scripts that use the character, providing the copyright ownership is clearly stated in all transactions.

23

Getting Ideas

An original idea is made up of unoriginal ideas seen in a different light. It is by taking the ordinary and accepted and saying "If we did this and this, what would happen then?" There are a number of ready-made methods that can be tried out for any situation.

Brainstorming. A group of people offer as many ideas as possible. No ideas are criticised. Each one is taken on its merits and pushed as far as it will go, and only rejected when a better approach is suggested.

Replacement. The characters in a well established story are replaced, but the story is kept essentially the same (typical of basic plots such as cowboys, crime, horror films, etc). One can also keep the characters and replace the story, eg: Robin Hood rides again.

Extension. A well established storyline is taken beyond the actual story. Walt Disney's *Snow White* does this by the addition of music, and giving the characters more personality. In effect it takes an existing story and makes it the basis for another one.

Context. A simple story can be changed by placing an element out of context: Tarzan is an English Lord put in the jungle; Tom Thumb is a normal boy in every way except scale. He tries to cope with a normal world. Such situations, where one element is changed gives us giants, witches, dwarfs, fairies, mermaids, ghosts, etc.

Transfer. An established storyline and characters is transferred to another situation. Cowboys transfer to science fiction adventures. Shakespeare plots transfer to big business. In animation people are transformed into animals, but all else remains the same.

Reversal. Roles in a story are reversed. Kings become beggars and kitchen maids princesses. The dual side of our personality is explored so that the Jekyll and Hyde aspect becomes the ugly toad who is a handsome prince.

Renovation. Take an existing story and see if it can be improved. Fairy tales are ideal for this.

Abstraction. Take the key characters from a story and build another story around them, eg: The ugly sisters of Cinderella are given a story that excludes Cinderella.

Combination. Use parts of several stories and combine them. A good example is King Kong: a tribal god, extended in scale, in a lost world, out of context (jungle to New York) with a Beauty and beast theme (Show Biz and the air battle as throw-away extras).

BASIC STORY APPROACHES

A. Replacement. Robin Hood story using animal characters. B. Transfer. Tycoon and Corporation building to King and Castle. C. Renovation. Aesops fables updated with modern characters. D. Abstraction. Wizard of Oz used as a basic character for other stories.

Getting More Ideas

There are many ideas around just begging to be made into films. One very rich field is in 'readers letters' columns in magazines and newspapers. They all express attitudes in a brief way on subjects of interest.

The letters fall into three broad groups:

1. Letters asking for advice. The use of the newspaper is incidental as an adviser.

2. Writing in relation to something that has been printed in the particular paper. This, in some way, identifies with the paper – even if going against the views printed. It may well be part of a continuing dialogue.

3. To publicise views to the world. Here the newspaper is being used as a platform.

It is the *way* the ideas are expressed that is important. It gives a vital clue to the sort of values and background of a person expressing them. Imagine a confrontation between person 'A' writing 'Dear sir, I believe that unofficial strikers should be horsewhipped.' And person 'B' writing 'Dear Sir, I have pimples, scraggy hair, buck teeth, and knock knees. What chance of success do I have in life?'

Try to write such examples of letters by copying the phrasing and sentence length. Count the average number of words in a sentence, and pick out the emotive words.

Try to visualise the sort of people who would write such letters, and imagine the sort of replies they would get.

Letters as an art form
Letters sum up ideas just as films do. Practising letter writing is one of the best methods of learning to set out an idea clearly and simply. Pick out several papers and journals that appear to a cross section of society, and see how many letters you can get printed. Always keep a packet of postcards handy for doing this, and give yourself a target such as getting twenty printed in a year; even replying to your own letters if necessary.

LETTERS AS STORY IDEAS

Visualising the authors of letters. Try to imagine how each would react to a similar situation.

Stereotypes

It is not the name but the attributes that define a character. As most animation films are short, you need to define your characters quickly and clearly. For this you need basic stereotypes for reference. The stereotypes fall into three broad groups:

Situations. Where it can be seen at a glance what has, is, or is about to happen.

Attributes. Where it is evident how two characters or groups are relating to each other.

Individuals. Where what they are is made evident by their clothes, accessories, age, manner, etc.

Examples of situations might be:

War. The sight of a plane and the sudden action-stations panic.

Science fiction. The spaceman suddenly coming face to face with the monster.

Gunfight. The cowboy kicking open the bar door and swaggering in. In these cases it is the environment and action that define the situation. The situations are reinforced by the clothes and reactions of the characters, and then further stated by the resolution of the situation depending on the attributes of the characters concerned.

Relationships

These can be conveniently put into three groups – the dominant figure, the equal figure, and the subdominant figure. These in turn form two relationships: two characters on equal terms, or two characters with one being dominant such as parent-child, boss-employee, performer-audience or leader-follower, etc. Conflicts arise when the roles are not clear cut. Two men may vie for leadership to take the dominant role, or one finds leadership forced upon him because others refuse to accept responsibility (taking the subdominant role). The searching for a role, or basis for a working relationship is fundamental to all stories.

Attributes can be separated into positive and negative: beautiful-ugly, rich-poor, healthy-ill, clever-stupid, experienced-naive, strong-weak, influential-powerless, charming-boring, witty-dull, etc.

These attributes can be juxtaposed to create an imbalance that may later be resolved.

Beautiful-poor . . . Cinderella.

Charming-stupid . . . Dopey of the seven dwarfs.

Strong-powerless . . . Samson in chains.

The attributes are reinforced by addition: Rich-beautiful-clever. Poor-ugly-weak.

Animated characters should be quite unambiguous in their ages, attributes, roles, and endpoints. These elements must be clearly stated in the script.

CREATING CLICHES

A. Stereotypes. (1) Cliché cowboy. (2) Cliché spaceman and monster. B.
Relationships. (1) Child/adult. (2) Equals. C. Attributes. (1) Big and stupid. (2) Weak
and clever.

Laugh, and the world laughs with you.

Categories of Humour

'Murphie's law' of humour states: 'If something can go wrong — it will'. If you survive the event it is comedy; if you don't, it's tragedy. It is upon this fine edge of survival that all drama rests. Survival means retaining or upgrading your position in some way. To do this by chance, or in some way out of context is an attribute of humour.

There are three broad categories of humour. All of them assume that the audience can identify the character and context to some extent — the greater the extent, the greater leeway for subtlety.

The first category is *saying* something funny. Spoken humour requires reflection upon what is said, so the situation has to be stated and established. If then, a punch line or deliberate un-resolution of the 'logical' storyline development follows, it will throw the mental images of the audience in disorder. The mental juxtaposition of real and anticipated ideas is the source of amusement.

A sense of 'correctness' is also inherent in spoken humour. A pun will appeal more to a person who uses words correctly; a religious joke will not appeal particularly to an atheist. The limitations of spoken humour do not, in general, make it suitable for animation because of its dependence upon the audience having the wrong mental images. But it can be used in animation where the images satirise the spoken word.

A more direct form of humour is *doing* something funny. This requires the context being well established with both characters and situation: a waiter with a loaded tray of custard tarts will certainly be expected to trip over, but the infinite ways in which this can be done prevent the audience from knowing how and when.

A study of silent films; especially classics with Buster Keaton, Harold Lloyd, Harry Lang, Laurel and Hardy, etc., will show how the audience can be led along to anticipate the wrong endpoint. The trick is often in the timing which uses the audiences' mental 'follow through' of a situation.

The audience can also be misled by ambiguous backgrounds, noises and images. But the danger is producing something that looks too contrived. There should always be an inherent logic implying a natural sequence of events that can be identified and to some extent taken for granted, otherwise the audience will subconsciously search for clues and lose the point of the humour.

More direct, but less subtle is *being* something funny. Clowns, for example, are out of context with the world yet try to be part of it. They are unaware, incongruous, and absurd, yet not essentially silly or stupid; and to a great extent their humour is dependent on the fact that they can cope or even win out against a normal person.

Humour must be derived naturally from the situation, which must not be 'bent' to suit the gag. Analyse every element and see what you can add or subtract so that a situation lends itself to manipulation.

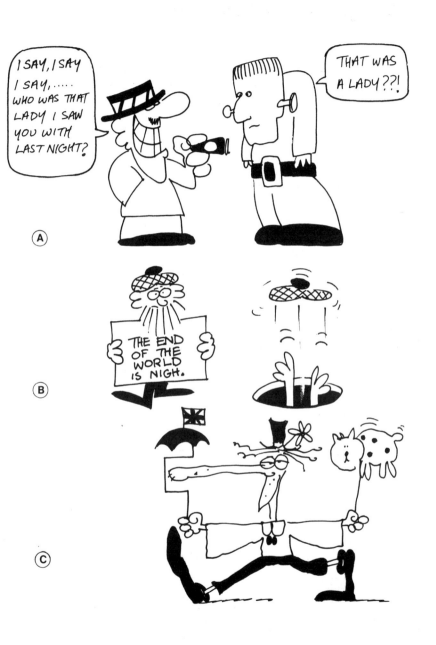

LEVELS OF HUMOUR

A. Saying something funny. B. Doing something funny. C. Being funny.

Diabolus ex machina.

Hostile World of Humour

Machines, furniture, tools, clothes, and toys are typical articles bent upon man's destruction: the unwary fall foul of them right through their lives. The inability to come to terms with the world we have created is the basis of a large realm of humour.

All mechanical objects can be reduced to a few basic principles — the wheel, wedge, lever, gear, inclined plane, pulley, roller, and spring. These are known as simple machines. Taking the principles of these machines and looking for them in everyday objects allows the most unlikely things to be used in a hostile way.

Wheels are anything that roll or turn. Anything that will roll away from you when dropped, or things that unexpectedly spin or turn.

Wedges are anything that can be jammed into openings at the wrong time: feet in doors, fingers in drawers/lids, tools into machinery, etc.

Levers are anything that gives an extra and unexpected turn of power to an object — the rake that hits you on the nose when trodden on, the loose plank or, the walking stick that gets caught in the door.

Gears are anything that revolve with the effect of tearing, flattening, or chewing up. Gears with chain drives have even more potential.

Inclined planes are any slope or uneven step that causes imbalance. Moving inclined planes, such as ship's decks, cause even more havoc.

Pulleys are anything that a rope, wire, or chain can get caught around to pull in the opposite direction to that required or expected. The ropes and wires usually have loops in them as ready-made traps.

Rollers are things that overcome friction and are likely to be stepped upon, eg: pencils, marbles, skates, toys, bottles.

Springs are things that give an unexpected recoil effect. Flexible planks, bars or rods. Any sort of rubberwear that can be caught up and stretched.

Means of operating
Apart from machines there are also the means and effects of operating them.

Gravity will cause anything to drop, bend, or roll when it shouldn't.

Lubrication includes oil, soap, polish, banana skins.

Hooks include anything protruding to catch on clothes, or triggering off accidently — knobs, handles, buttons, switches, buckles.

Safety devices cover all those things labelled 'Emergency', 'Don't touch', 'Danger', etc — Fire alarms, lifts, security warnings.

Tripping is the delight of wires, hoses, carpets, loose floorboards, toolboxes, toys, small animals, stairs.

Power feels best when abused. Electricity, steam, water jets, compressed air, fire, gas, unstable heavy weights.

A study of cartoons such as Tom and Jerry will show how these concepts can be transferred to make the most innocuous objects into lethal weapons.

MACHINES AS PROPS

A. Things for slipping on. B. Things to catch on. C. Things for tripping over. D. Things to fall down from or into. E. Power from electricity, steam, compressed air, water and gas.

33

Researching a Script

Philosophy

Every subject has a philosophy behind it. The man who designs dog biscuits will have as much involvement with his subject as the man who designs space ships. Getting a feeling for this philosophy is basic to understanding the subject — and eventually putting it across to the audience.

Let's say the subject is something like 'Catalysts in Oil Refineries'. The sponsors often supply plenty of material to read and a broad outline of what they want. But quite often the person you speak to is the public relations, or audio-visual man in the company, who may not know much more about the subject than you do. He may call in an expert — who has little idea about film making. It is better at this stage to view some of their previous films perhaps with their expert. Next, look through trade journals related to the subject noting cartoons, jokes, illustrations, and photos that seem relevant.

Reading through the article headings (and any brief synopses under them) quickly gives you a feeling for things related to the subject. The public relations department will have news clippings and their own press releases on company activities. Being presented for the general public, they will give an indication of how the company sees itself.

The company may also employ or know technical journalists who specialise in its own field. Talking to them, even over the phone, gives you a broad outline of the key points.

Facts

Once you have got a feeling for the subject and can see where it fits into the scheme of things, your reading of the factual material will be easier and more efficient. Write down every turn that seems to be a key point in describing what you are saying, and then try to get a visual interpretation of this. It will not matter if this is a simple diagram to begin with.

When you have enough key points to make sense of the various stages, draw up a simple flow chart that puts these points in order, eg:

1. Description of a catalyst — Would the audience know this?
2. Particular type of catalyst used. — Are there a variety of them?
Are there various products?
3. How is it used for the particular product — Is this a major point?
4. How is the product used.

By questioning the points you put down, you can see other areas and extensions of your research. Each point should be questioned until the final answer is one that offers simple visual explanation.

34

RESEARCHING SCRIPTS

Check libraries for source books and magazines.

Contact authors of books and articles for leads and approaches.

First look for illustrations. Copy, cut out and trace off wherever possible.

Note important points.

Separate facts and attitudes.

Fact: 2 million tons of dog food is consumed each year.

Philosophy: Happy dogs make the world go round.

Adaptations from other Media

Many animated films are adaptations from books or comics. In many cases the material seems ideally suitable for adaptation. But consider the differences. Books can be read in private at the reader's own pace and referred back to if necessary, whereas films are shown under totally different conditions. Books are also presented to *make* the reader use his imagination, and to leave certain aspects open to interpretation – or even leave them unresolved.

Literal translations for animation never work. What has to be translated is the *mood and concept* of the book, and then reinforced with film techniques so that they come over even stronger than the book (if they do not then there is no point in making the film).

Typical problems that come up in translation are visual interpretations such as: 'She was the most beautiful princess in the world . . .' or 'Five hundred horsemen came galloping over the hill . . .' or 'The acid and alkali interact to form a salt and water'. The concept, action, or detail may not be practical to actually animate. On the other hand a phrase like 'Pooh stopped and thought for a while . . .' might lend itself to a very funny visual interpretation.

When translating a book, go through it looking for the strongest visual elements either as described in the book, or as you imagine them. See how these elements can be reinforced by the addition of sound and movement. Check how your interpretation fits in with that of others who have read the book.

Quite often an idea in a book requiring several characters can be reduced to one character. In technical books it is common to use analogies where a film might use a simplified version of an actual process.

Sometimes an adaptation might be made from several books of a series and have these condensed into one film. You pick the best characters from each book and adapt the storyline to link these consistently with the story as a whole. In adaptations that add music and voices, minor characters in the book often take on a bigger role in the film.

Cartoon strips

The most difficult thing to do when translating cartoon strips to film is to find a suitable voice, as this may give a definition of class and background that are not always evident in the strip. Once you have the voice, this will, to some extent, indicate other defining characteristics.

A film contains far more background illustration and props than a strip. So search the strip for as many clues as possible, to give an overall consistency that can be reinforced. Otherwise the characters may lose their proper context. Most cartoon characters are built around a single human idiosyncrasy. Make sure you have defined this clearly enough to react consistently in various situations.

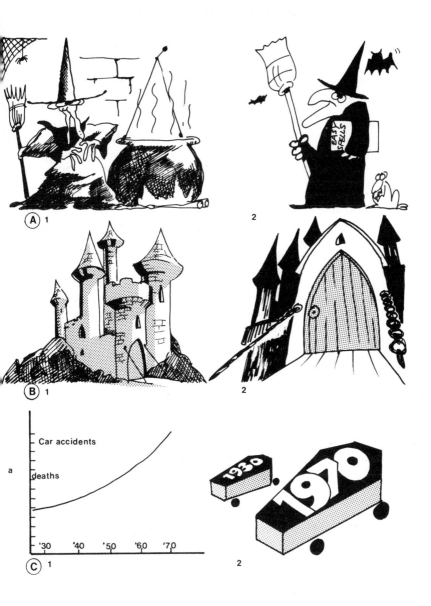

TRANSLATING STILLS TO ANIMATION

A. Design. (1) Book character with the atmosphere created by detail. (2) Animation character. Simpler, with atmosphere reinforced by secondary characters. B. Angles. (1) Graphic view presents information. (2) Filmic view creates drama. C. Visualisation. (1) To be read with text in a book. (2) To be read for impact in a film.

37

Learning by Looking

Silent films
The early silent comedies (tragedies never worked as well) come very close to the ideal guide for animation. They are normally confined to three basic shot types: Close Up, Mid Shot, and Long Shot (distant) (see SHOTS . . .) have very little editing; and quite clearly establish the situation with every possible cliché and prop possible. Over and above this, they use timing to perfection. (See Timing the Storyboard.)

While watching silent films, mentally analyse what is being done. Note the camera shots, and try to guess what will happen. After a while you will see that a few tricks can be given many disguises by being placed in a different context. If the silent film has a piano accompaniment, then note the sort of musical clichés that set the scene.

TV and Radio
Watching TV with the sound turned off shows how little of the action comes over without sound. Again, if you close your eyes and listen to the sound, it is difficult to follow. This is because TV (live, not a film made for the cinema), like a stage presentation, deals mainly in human situations where non-verbal communication of gestures and body movement is integrated with the dialogue.

Radio is closer to the book 'form' and makes greater demands upon the audience's imagination. It is easy to follow a radio play without putting too much thought into what the players look like, or what the backgrounds are supposed to be. Sound effects and 'aural backgrounds' are useful in animation and allow impossible situations to be created, eg: a man being washed down a sink plughole, musical instruments that speak.

Children's stories adapted for radio are almost ready-made for animation. Try to think of a sound track in these terms.

Mime and circuses
Where the presentation does not depend upon sound, or where it is an extra, as in mime and the circus, then forms establish themselves immediately in visual terms.

The exaggerated movements of the mimic, and well established dress of circus artists need no further interpretation. Analyse why certain characteristics come over so strongly, also, what is so interesting about a circus when virtually everything about it can be anticipated. One aspect is that they deal in concepts pushed to their human limits . . . animation takes over from that point.

FORMATS OF OTHER MEDIA

A. Comics. Analyse shots and framings used in comics. B. Silent films and the stage.
Setting the scene with simple props.

39

Defining Concepts

Animation is, above all else, a conceptual medium. It deals with ideas and their associations rather than concrete incidents. Concepts are often difficult to define except by giving examples and analogies. The first definition to look for is the 'class' it falls into, and then give other examples of this class. Let's take a horse as an example:

Horse (classed as cattle) . . . cows and sheep.
Horse (classed as transport) . . . cars, bicycles.
Horse (classed as things to sit upon) . . . chairs, stools, cushions.
Horse (classed as cowboy's accessories) guns, lassos, spurs.

These concepts are used in play and design: chairs have been designed as saddles, and children play horses on anything they can sit astride.

This transfer of concepts is commonly exploited in animation, particularly in cartoons like Tom and Jerry where the most ingenious ways are used to bend the concepts. The associations fall into two groups: the *design* where things look alike, and the *function* where things fulfil a similar purpose.

Sequence: Cat in kitchen tries to catch mouse stealing food. He throws egg (missile) at the mouse. The mouse takes frying pan (tennis racket) and hits egg back. The concept has transferred to a tennis match. The scene is now open for bread rolls, fruit, vegetables, etc., to be used as tennis balls. There is also the parallel concept of a war, which could bring in using saucepans and kitchen utensils as tin hats and armour. This would then allow knives and forks to be used as spears. Eventually the kitchen furniture might be rearranged as a fortress.

By continually developing the transferable elements of something it is possible to animate anything as any other thing. The idea of similar elements is implicit in magic and superstitions and is a recurring theme in fairy tales.

Combining concepts

Combining concepts is a useful device in creating extraordinary beasts (mythology) and machines (science fiction). Many practical inventions are the results of combining apparently unrelated ideas in a novel way. Some such Victorian inventions appear ridiculous to us today because the concepts of the time are no longer with us.

The visual concept can be reinforced very effectively by sound. If a mouse hits a cat over the head with a dinner gong hammer, the cat should both sound and vibrate like a gong. If the cat is hit with a sledge hammer then it would be driven into the ground like a pile.

Once the viewer's mind has accepted the transfer, then the stage is set for a series of situations based upon this. But don't let any sequence go on long enough for the audience to guess what is coming, nor let any situation be the result of a contrived transfer.

40

ANALYSING CONCEPTS

A. Classes. Associations with a horse. B. Concept transfer. Tennis racquet and ball or frying pan and egg, extended to 'kitchen armoury'. C. Combined concepts. An umbrella visually transfers to a parachute or boat.

Association of Ideas

Whereas concepts can be classified with common elements, an associated idea may not have any direct link. Flowers remind one person of a loved one, but another of hayfever. The links are there, but they vary from person to person. It is these hidden links that give us our reference points and attitudes to life. When you explore the connections with a subject, look both for the obvious links, and the more subtle ones. Take, for example, the simple case of a rainbow:

Shape: A rainbow is semi-circular. Could it be circular, square, or shaped like a person?

Colour: It is multi-coloured. Could it be in tones of one colour, or just black and white?

Dimension: It appears two dimensional. Could it be three dimensional like a hemisphere?

Design: The colours are parallel with each other. Could they be interwoven, or vertical, or dots and squiggles?

Structure: It looks like a bridge or an archway. Could it be used in this way? It also appears to come out of the ground. Could it grow like a tree?

Name: It is called *rainbow.* Could it be called 'sunbow', 'windbow', 'snowbow', 'moonbow', 'starbow', etc., and have closer links with these?

Composition: It is an illusion. Could it be solid and chopped down? Could it be plastic and bent around?

Size: They appear to be huge. Could they be small?

Number: They appear singly. Could they appear by the hundred?

Parallels: There are seven colours. Could these be linked to the seven days of the week, the seven notes of the scale, the seven deadly sins?

Sensory factors: We only see them. Could they be touched, smelt, heard, tasted?

Exploring an idea like this might be to take the suggestion of 'snowbow', and have all the snowflakes different colours. Once this has been established then other ideas will come from the association. Look up descriptions of even obvious words in the dictionary and thesaurus. These will give leads for further associations.

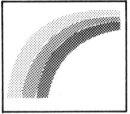
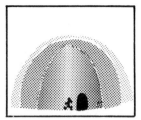

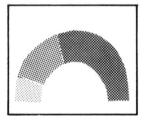
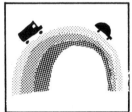
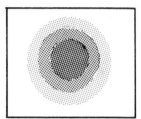

EXTENDING CONCEPTS

Rainbow concepts: Shape, colour, dimension, design, structure, name (sunbow), composition, size and number, parallels.

Story Aims

A good start to a story means gaining the audience's interest right away and establishing the mood and direction of the film. The end of the film should also somehow be implicit in the beginning.

It is a basic law of nature that all things tend to resolve to their most stable state, and this is generally true of stories: in fact the unfolding of the resolution *is* the story. The two simplest forms of story upon which all others are built are: Stable state ... unstable state ... stable state, and Unstable state ... stable state.

Of course, the story will not *simply* resolve, but will have various twists and turns so that the known resolution (that which is expected or stated) is achieved against obvious expectations, or the assumed resolution turns out to be different from the one anticipated. The resolution can be unstated and only made known at the end. Here are a few routine situations that use these patterns.

Stable-unstable-stable
Crime occurs ... everyone suspected ... crime solved.
Town is peaceful ... trouble comes ... trouble goes.
Boy finds girl ... boy loses girl ... boy finds girl.

Unstable-stable
Person unfulfilled ... finds fulfilment
Person in trouble ... person gets out of trouble
Group in danger ... group finds salvation.

There are obviously counterpoint states of stability/instability in each sequence to stop the resolution coming too quickly or neatly. The sort of things that prevent early resolution, or throw a spanner in the works, are to have unexpected barriers, eg: The mechanical barriers may be overcome but the psychological ones still remain. Or the gain of one means the loss of another.

Finding a balance
The quest of the characters must be roughly equal to their capabilities, otherwise the story becomes contrived. For Winnie the Pooh, finding honey just about stretches his capabilities to the limit, whereas the most complex crime would hardly be a match for Sherlock Holmes.

The originality of a story will come from finding ways of achieving the end points within the logical and acceptable capabilities of the characters.

Try to analyse the elements needed to attain a given end point. To chase Moby Dick required a whaling ship, and a fanatical determination, whereas Popeye only requires a tin of spinach to achieve anything he wants.

ANALYSING RELATIONSHIPS

A. Resolving unstable states. B. Positive and negative elements.

Realm of the Impossible

Animation is the art of possible worlds, but more truly the art of impossible worlds. Elephants fly, and rabbits talk. Human foibles and idiosyncrasies are seen more clearly when transferred to animals and objects. Galaxies are stopped in their motion, and atoms presented the size of footballs to put them into our scale of comprehension. Yet, in spite of every distortion in size, shape, colour, movement, and context, the ideas come over more strongly than in reality. The binding force that contains these elements in a recognisable form is *logic*.

The laws of the universe are constant and indestructable, and are intuitively recognised even in the most abstract forms. And it is this that allows magic to be credible. Good fairies can never beat bad fairies by magic alone; it also takes planning, cunning and timing, in fact an analogy of power in the real world. There is also the transference of attributes 'as like to like'. It is far more acceptable too, for a pumpkin and six mice to be made into a coach and horses than to produce the goods by a click of the thumb.

Physical laws of unknown worlds

Little men from outer space may have three eyes, four legs, and sparkle, but they are still bound by the laws of gravity, action and reaction, etc. If they are invulnerable to bullets then there are explainable reasons for this. If they are super intelligent, there will be evidence of this too. If they are highly civilised then it will show in their arts and humour as well as their technology. It is not good enough to take human attributes and dress them up in weird shapes to pass off as other creatures. The logic has to follow through to show what they have in common with humans and what definable differences they have, eg: would a man with three eyes have to have two noses to balance his spectacles? Or would bicycles exist in a world of three legged people? It is the sum effect of these differences that make the unknown world different, rather than bizarre distortions of our own world.

The physical laws of the known world

Although animation normally bends the physical laws of nature to the point of unacceptance, it is also common to bend them to appear acceptable. It is common to show underwater scenes as very colourful, but apart from very shallow depths, there is little colour to be seen underwater. It has also become accepted to have the deep inhabited by dangerous tentacled and sharp toothed beasts, yet there is considerably more danger in the innocuous looking but highly poisonous shells, plants, and fish that simply lie in wait for the unwary. Some familiarity with the worlds you write about is essential if you are to explore the possibilities of extending the physical laws for the super-reality of animation.

VISUAL LOGIC

A. If pigs could fly, they would obey the same laws of flight as birds do. B. Balance of power between good and bad characters. C. Common attributes are the basis for understanding other creatures. D. Magic is 'a state of change', not the creation of something from nothing.

Communicating

There are three levels of communication that we use all the time:
1. *Communicating with ourselves* in the way we think about things.
2. *Communicating with the people we know.* The roles we play and responses we make to the people we are involved with.
3. *The way we communicate with the world generally.* Being the sort of image we put on; the attitudes and manners we take on, and the sort of company we seek.

Everyone is two-sided at least, and we only show one facet of our nature at a time. It is the revealing of the other facets of our character that gives us depth.

In animation it is very easy to present these aspects of people so that they communicate the sort of ideas intended, but most animation characters are rather flat because the underlying feelings are not revealed. In *Snow White,* the two sides of the Beautiful Queen/Wicked Witch give her a lot more depth than Snow White herself.

By making characters 'think' on the screen, the audience identifies with them more. The pauses, hesitations, and gestures of confidence indicate the person behind the image. Getting an animated character to become a personality means developing him in the same way as a playwright would for a real person. This requires seeing the sort of things he identifies with, the sort of friends he would have the things that would amuse and upset him.

A study of advertising pictures shows how the backgrounds, props, dress, drinks, and postures communicate ideas about the character.

Identity
Everyone is looking for identity in some way or other. We may have a sense of what we are, in which case we will try to project that image. On the other hand, we may be given an identity by others by means of a nickname or the way they approach us. Look at people and see if you can guess their job or interests by the way they dress, move, stand, talk, etc. Also look for inconsistent features that show another side of their character, eg: someone who dresses like a hippie but does so with very expensive clothes.

Identifying the characters in a story means being able to think of them as people you know.

NON-VERBAL COMMUNICATION

A. Communicating with ourselves, directly with another and with the world as a whole. B. A miser likes to see himself as clever, but by his colleagues as hard-working and by the world as poor. C. The Jekyll and Hyde in us all visually exploited as two versions of the same person.

49

Enough is as good as a feast (proverb).

Limits of Information

To be of value, information has to *inform* — to tell you something you didn't already know. So in spite of the ability to put on an unlimited amount of information, the limits are what the viewer can take in.

One soldier walking will be accepted as one moving object. A battalion of soldiers marching will be accepted as one moving object. Even two armies fighting will be accepted as one moving object, once the pattern is set. But let one soldier stop fighting and start picking daisies, then there are two patterns, each having a different 'information content'. It is not what is actually happening on the screen in terms of physical movement, but what is going on. In the above case there is a war going on in one place, and a soldier picking daisies in another, each vieing for the viewer's attention. When the war pattern has been established, the daisy-picking becomes 'unresolved information' that has to be established by the viewer saying 'what's going on . . . oh, a soldier has got fed up with the war and is picking daisies' . . . once that is established the viewer will look for more information.

Optical illusions
The reason that optical illusions are interesting is that they seem to give you information, but when you test it by checking the other clues, you find that there is either not enough, or too much information — so that it is open to several interpretations. This type of ambiguity can be used in animation so that the viewer is never quite sure what is happening until the situation is resolved by adding the relevant information.

The flow of information is not the same as the flow of movement. Something may be moving very busily but gives no further information once its purpose is established, whereas a still object (like a painting) might have a considerable amount of information coming from it as the viewer's eye interprets and relates the various elements.

Viewer's interest is sustained by controlling the flow of information so that there is never too much, or too little, going on. But as the assimilating rate of audience differs, the 'rapid' viewer can be kept in check by inserting counterpoint movements, gags, and embellishments. These are throwaway lines or effects that, if taken, will add to the film, but if missed, will not detract from the main content.

Typical of such gags is to have notices, graffiti, caricatures, absurd props, and cliché situations as backgrounds that quietly fill the space and which, if given a glance, will make the scene richer.

Check what the eye can take in by looking at a picture for a few seconds and then closing your eyes to see what can be remembered, and why you remembered it.

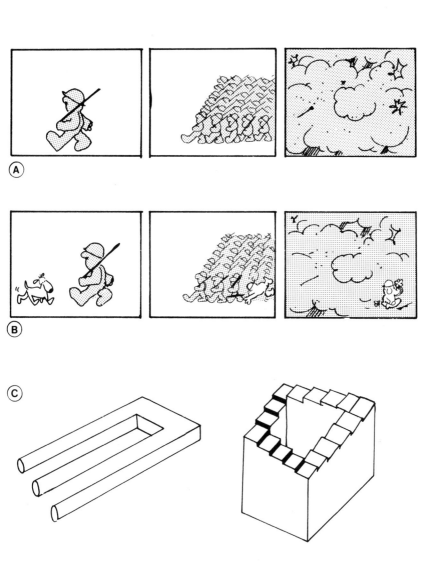

ISOLATING INFORMATION

A. One soldier, a battalion or even a battle is seen as one movement. B. Another character or inconsistent movement will split the scene. C. Optical illusions give too little or too much information to enable the viewer to resolve them rationally.

All the world's a stage.

Associated Media

Animation technique embraces a bag of optical tricks that have been added to by people who noticed that certain effects would have useful applications. Many of these effects were developed for displays, advertising or live demonstrations. Others were chance observations related to animation.

As a rough guide, anything that catches the eye as an effect, could possibly be used in animation. The places to look for such effects are in processes such as printing, photography, art forms, electronic displays, computer printouts and plots, copying techniques and so on. Quite often the effects are achieved in a simple way such as by projecting on to a screen that is coloured, uneven, semi-transparent, reflective, slotted or even moving — such as sheets of water or dancing people. Other effects can be achieved by using colours that are fluorescent or containing glittering particles.

New directions
It is fairly easy to predict new developments in principle, if not in detail. Generally speaking, black and white images move to colour. Still images are given movement. Silent images are given sound. Two-dimensional images go to three-dimensional. Single images go to multiple images, etc., so that the gap closes between the image and the reality that it portrays.

Image processing
Film making can be classified as one aspect of information processing, where data is 'captured', stored, displayed, manipulated and recorded. The three broad areas of film, video, and computer techniques are continually merging to the common end of having complete control over the image processing. Each technique has inherent advantages and disadvantages that have come about by the type of information they are designed to handle. Studying and analysing this aspect reveals that type of information might be extended, explored, and adapted for other techniques.

The techniques not only lend themselves to animated films; animated films lend themselves to the techniques. Landing a spaceship on the moon required simulation techniques that were, effectively, animation. The moving contours of a weather map are animation. The 'stop' and 'go' traffic signs on the road are a limited form of animation. Do not think of animation as being restricted to the screen, or even having a storyline. By thinking of the world as a 'screen' you will see countless examples of essentially animated techniques around you. This way of thinking makes it easier to translate otherwise complex ideas into everyday terms.

Neon signs and advertising displays.

Video display units and indicator
boards.

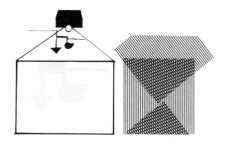

Kinetic art and moiré patterns.

Fibre optics and slide projectors.

Great minds think alike.

Related Art Forms

Although the basic interests of life are few, there are many ways of expressing the comedies and tragedies that beset us. It is valuable to compare different art forms that attempt to express the same ideas, and see how these can be used in combination for the multimedia art form of film.

Photography
A good photograph can catch the unique moment or mood that sums up the situation. This statement may then be reinforced by processing, framing, and being plated in context with other photographs or words.

Acting
The difficulty of acting is to 'be natural', which in practice means being very unnatural by communicating ideas simply and clearly. This is done by eliminating all the movements, speech, and obstacles that detract from what is being conveyed and then reinforcing the positive ideas with emphasis, and directing these at the audience as well as the other actors.

Dancing
Using space and time with music and movement comes very close to animation. Watch how movements on one part of the stage can reinforce movements on the other. Abstract animation can often be thought of as a dance.

Drawing and painting
The eye looks for sense rather than detail, this is why abstract paintings can often create a mood more forcefully than do representational works. It is very common in animation to use abstract backgrounds that suggest ideas rather than state them explicitly.

Music
Music can support mental images and carry them along. It is much easier to put pictures to music than to put music to pictures. A feeling for music greatly helps in timing and creating a mood for animation, particularly with animation cycles that risk being boring.

Summary
Animation is a derived art form. It depends almost entirely upon the acceptance of other art forms and the conventions that go with them. Try to analyse animation in terms of its various elements and see how they complement each other. This will eventually lead to being able to conceive ideas as a whole.

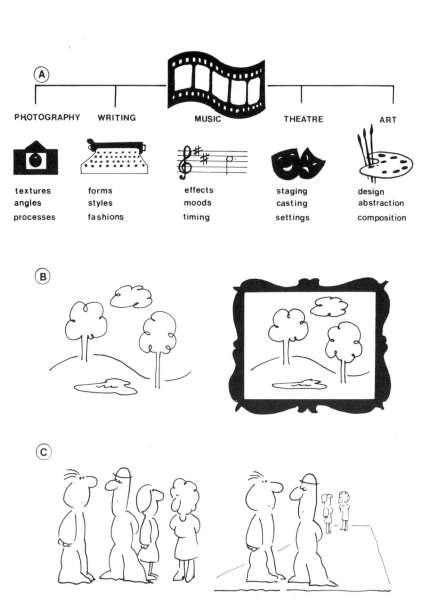

A
PHOTOGRAPHY   WRITING   MUSIC   THEATRE   ART

textures   forms   effects   staging   design
angles   styles   moods   casting   abstraction
processes   fashions   timing   settings   composition

B

C

BACKGROUND TO ANIMATION

A. Related artforms. B. Framing focuses the image. C. Staging puts key characters in a dominant position.

Honesty is the best policy.

Ethics and responsibility

In this case 'honesty' is simply being practical about what you can do in a given time at a given cost. As the writer comes in at the beginning of a film, many ideas are put forward that do not come to fruition, and at any time he might be actively working on several films without knowing which will eventually go into production, or when. Sooner or later two jobs will appear with the same priorities or deadlines. He then has four choices:

1. Refusing one of the jobs (this may be difficult if you are the one who has done the groundwork on it).
2. Accepting both jobs, but with the clear understanding that one must be given a lower priority.
3. Accepting both jobs, but sharing the work, where possible, with another writer.
4. Accepting both jobs but not doing your best on either of them.

It is very common for clients to give phoney deadlines assuming that this will give them a working margin if something goes wrong. It is also common for producers to assume that any given deadline can be extended once the film is in production. It is much easier for all concerned if practical and realistic time scales can be given and kept to. To do this it is a good idea to give estimates on each stage of the storyboard — outline, treatment, rough, storyboard, final storyboard (see page 12), with a minimum and maximum date saying 'We cannot possibly do it before such a date, but will guarantee it by such a date at the latest'. If snags prevent these dates being kept to, then the client should be kept informed about the situation voluntarily. Otherwise, with any suspicion on the client's side you will be constantly bothered and made to produce work in an uncreative climate.

Who does what?
Advertising agencies might do their own storyboards and give these to a studio to be 'tidied up'. Or the writer might work with the producer, director or animator at the ideas stage of the film. This is fine if it is understood who is supposed to be doing what, and who actually does it. It is possible to start out with a good idea, spend the day discussing and altering it and then end up with the same idea. In effect, nothing has been added. But time and effort has been taken in a worthwhile cause if it has proved the soundness of the original idea. It can also happen that after much exploratory work on the part of one person, another may just hit on the right aspect, to pull the ideas together and claim the ideas as his — so write all your ideas down.

In conclusion, always make sure that you know what you are expected to do, in what time, for what payment. Do not take on work which you do not have the time, experience, or interest to fulfil competently. If the final film fails, everyone but you can blame the script.

	JAN.		FeD.		March.		
outline	▓						
treatment		▓					
storyboard rough.			▓				
final STORYBOARD					▓	▓	

Give estimates on each stage of the storyboard.

Be honest.

Keep notes, sketches and recordings on all ideas used for future reference.

57

Drawn, cutouts, and models.

Styles and Techniques

Animation is defined as *any* film that is shot frame-by-frame, but it is convenient to think of animation as any film that is *not* live-action, as even live-action shooting of effects tends to go to animation studios.

All animation techniques are broadly based upon the three basic methods, drawing, cutouts, and models. There are many variations on each method, and sometimes methods are combined.

Drawn animation
This covers any method that requires drawing skill to make the image move. In effect it means that a new image is created for every movement.

The greatest benefit of drawn animation is that it allows the animator total control over the final image. It can easily be combined with live-action, photos, and other forms of artwork. It can be built up with layers of drawings to give a sense of depth, and allows the unique animation element of having one image change into another. Its disadvantages include the high cost and long time taken to produce a film by this method.

Cutout animation
A cutout can be any flat piece of material that may be moved around under the camera. Cardboard figures and photos are common. The advantage of this form of animation is that it is quick, relatively cheap, and much simpler than drawn animation, making it a suitable medium for low cost films, or amateur film makers. In the hands of a good designer it can be very effective but it lacks flowing movements, perspective, and the facility of being easily combined with live-action film.

Model animation
This covers any method where a 3D object is moved around. This might be on a table, but can be done at several levels making it suitable for special effects. The techniques include clay modelling, wire figures, articulated models (King Kong) and various types of puppet. This kind of animation does not use an animation stand, but still requires a single-frame camera.

With this technique it is possible to use people as models to create crazy or magical effects. This is probably the simplest form of animation there is.

Cel animation.

Cut-out animation.

Model animation.

Clay, sand and string animation.

Animating by Machine

Live action films often need animated effects added to them after they have been shot. this can be done on an optical printer which is, in effect, a camera combined with a projector so that the projected film goes straight into the camera. By putting masks and filters between the two, and adding or subtracting frames to be shot, the original film can have a whole range of effects added, including the superimposition of new images, such as titles.

Typical of such effects would be to have a single frame of the original picture shot as a fading sequence to create a trailing image in different colours.

Rotoscoping
By projecting a live-action image on to a screen and tracing off the part you want, you end up with a series of drawings that are already animated for movement, but might have new colours or backgrounds added to them. This method is also used to add animation to a live-action film. The animation is drawn around the traced outline then, when shot over it, will be exactly registered.

Travelling matte
Another way to superimpose animation over live-action is to shoot the animation sequence with a black background and put the developed animation in the camera along with an unexposed roll of film upon which the live action is then printed. The live action is only copied on the unexposed parts of the film-leaving the outline of the animation to be registered together later.

Chroma key
Although not truly an animation technique, effectively the same method is used in putting animation over live-action on video tape. The animation is shot with a blue background (other colours are sometimes used providing they are very pure) and the live action and animation are mixed together electronically.

Cybernetic films
This covers any film that uses the characteristics of the machine for its styling. It includes video, optical, computers, mechanical, and even chemical means for generating artwork and patterns. These techniques are useful but should only be used where the technique is consistent with the message or styling of the overall film; used on their own they become a boring indulgence.

NON-ANIMATED EFFECTS

Titles, texts and masks overlaid.

Travelling mattes (film) and
Chroma-key (video) can combine
animation and live action. Animated
bird with painted background.

Live action component shot against
special background.

Combined effect.

Animation Movements

Animation movements are a combination of the animator's drawings, the movement of the camera, and the movement of the table. The animators movements cover any change in shape, where a new drawing is required to convey the change.

When the shape of the picture remains the same but there is a change in *scale,* then this can be done by the camera zooming in and out. The actual size of the screen remains the same, but the field of vision is made larger or smaller – so a small field shows less of the complete image but it is larger in relation to the screen size. A typical instruction might be 'Zoom into man's head' to show a close up of his face.

A change in *position* can be one of two things for the writer. Either it means that a particular image is actually moving over the screen, eg: 'A man walks across the screen', or, it means that an image appears to move, eg: 'walking man passes shops'. In this case the man would remain in the centre of the screen and the shops would be part of the moving background. The first case would be described as a man walking across the screen whereas the second case would be described as 'camera pans along with man walking'.

It must be remembered that movements in animation have no parallel with movements in the real world, and that the rate at which things move has to be thought out at the script stage. There is no way of working out at what speed a galaxy should explode, but given this as a subject, it would have to be considered in terms of what is being said and how long it takes for the information to be understood. The use of animation movements is to continually bring the relevant information into the screen at the rate it can be assimilated. No movement should be used for the sake of itself, nor should movements conflict with each other by straining the viewer's eye either by speed or location.

As a general rule, every movement should lead to new information, and stop when that information has been reached. This rule can be considered on the merits of each case, but remember too little movement is boring, and too much is confusing.

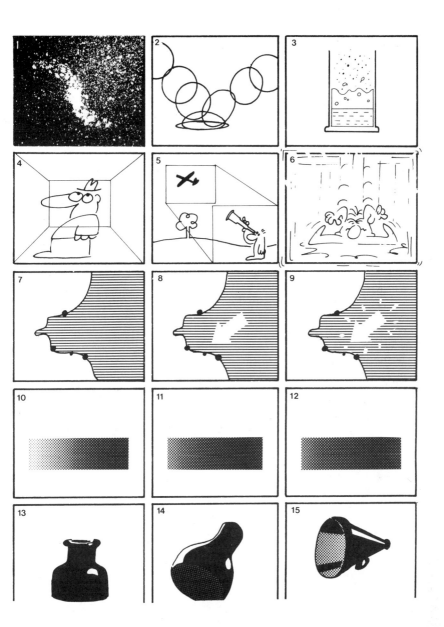

VISUALISING STATES OF CHANGE

Change of states. 1. Speeding up a galaxy. 2. Slowing down a bouncing ball. 3. Visualising water vapourising. 4. Zoom in. 5. Pan. 6. Camera shake to show impact. 7, 8, 9. Pop-on arrow and flash. 10, 11, 12. Dissolving to show cooling effect. 13, 14, 15. Metamorphosis.

63

Design Techniques

A good design works because it is simple to remember and provides a cue or mnemonic to identify with. It is useful to study books of symbols and signs to see how much information you can get from them, and if they trigger off the message they intend.

Scaling
Cartoon characters generally have disproportionately large heads, hands, and eyes because these are the features that convey the most information; they are the 'working' parts of the design. In a character that played football it might be useful to have very large feet. Make sure that the working parts are dominant.

Simplifying
There should never be a dot, line, colour, or movement on the screen that is not working for you. Start out with the simplest shapes possible that convey your intent, and then only add to this image where it gives reinforcement.

Abstracting
Some images, such as the human body, cannot always be simplified and remain meaningful. This is often the case in technical films where certain functions have to be demonstrated as accurately as possible. This problem can sometimes be overcome by abstracting the 'working' part and animating this, eg: The heart may be shown in context of the body, then abstracted and shown working as a pump. Once the principle has been shown the heart can be put back in context.

Highlighting
Even when a picture has been reduced to its essential parts it will still be necessary to convey the working parts by reinforcing them — by highlighting those parts with colour, toning down the background, flashing, outlining, or moving to the centre of the field. Any means of making this the focal point should be considered.

Superimposition
Superimposing means putting another image over an existing one. This might be a temporary device such as an arrow to indicate a particular piece of information. It could be a simplified drawing laid over the photograph of the real thing. It is a way of replacing or adding to an image that does not convey information simply enough for the context. A common use in advertising is to show a cut-away shot of a live-action object and have an animated sequence superimposed to demonstrate the concept or details of what otherwise would be difficult to show.

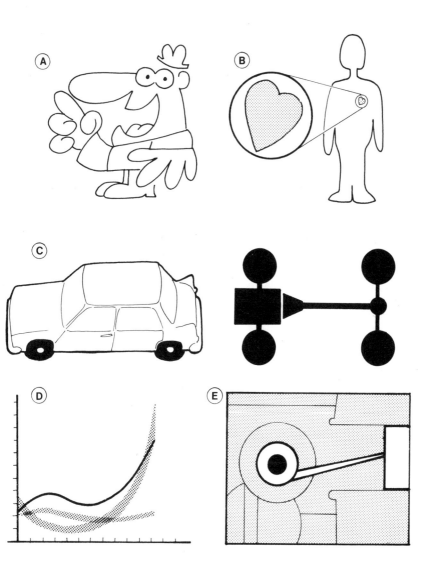

REINFORCING SIGNIFICANT INFORMATION

Design: A. Scaling up features with the most expression. B. Show in context, then extract detail. C. Simplify to significant parts. D. Superimpose new elements for comparison. E. Insignificant parts half-faded to emphasise important parts but still keep them in context.

Transitions

A transition shows the end of one scene and the beginning of another. It is comparable to punctuation, and shows to what degree each scene is related to the next.

Fade means fading off the image altogether – usually to black. It is like the break between paragraphs. A whole statement has been made, and there is a feeling of resolution.

Mix: (sometimes called a *Dissolve.*) This means fading off one scene while fading on another. Described on the script as 'Mix through to . . .'. In animation it is common to use a mix instead of a zoom because a close up shot may have more detailed artwork in it than one on a larger field. A mix is particularly useful when going from a real photo to a drawing of the photo and then into animation.

Wipe: means in effect wiping off the old scene and replacing it with the new one. It gives the sense that the things are happening concurrently. Although rarely used in animated films, most wipes for live-action films are animated patterns, and can be of any complexity. It is even common to use wipes for part of a scene so that the screen is divided up into sections and each part is changed independently – a technique often used for titles.

Flip: means having a board that spins vertically or horizontally so that the last piece of artwork from one scene is flipped round to bring on the first piece of artwork for the next scene which then goes into animation. This transition has a strong sense of continuity, and can be effectively used within a scene. There are ways of producing a flip electronically that extend its range of application.

Cut: this is the most abrupt way of going from one image to another. It has great visual impact, and quick cuts can give a very dramatic sense of movement to images that are otherwise statics, so it is often used where a sequence has many graphics (cutout and montage techniques). The cut can be reinforced well with sound effects.

Transitions within scenes
Because animation allows images to be changed as artwork, it is not necessary to have the range of transitions used in live-action, and the fade, mix, and cut cover most needs. But it is also possible in animation to use these transitions within the scene so that effects of mixing different parts of the image on and off at different rate can create flowing effects. These extensions should be considered as they add to the medium.

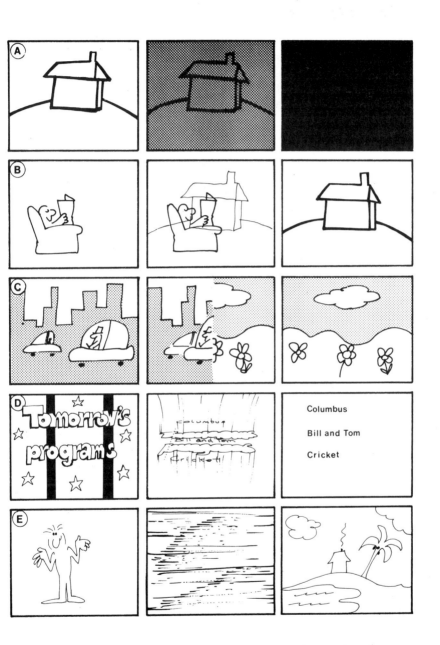

CHANGING SCENES

A. Fade out. B. Mix or dissolve. C. Wipe. D. Flip. E. Zip pan.

The Use of Colour

Next to movement, colour is the most dominant element of animation, and bright colours with hard edges are very characteristic of the medium. But it is often due to the bright colours that animation becomes hard on the eyes after a short while. Although there are no rules for using colours correctly, there are guides that help in a choice:

1. It is better to use the bright colours for the moving and key images rather than backgrounds and incidental animation.

2. The foreground colours should not clash with those in the background otherwise this gives a sense of flatness with the foreground sliding over the background.

3. When bright colours need to be used on static images, they can be subdued with textural effects.

4. If 'colour coding' is used to identify an element, eg: blue for water in a chemical reaction, then the coding must be retained throughout the film, and not used in a decorative or ambiguous way.

5. If colour is used to gain attention, as when flashing several colours on a logo or lettering, use only one colour when the flashing stops as multi-coloured text is extremely difficult to read.

6. Do not use colours as a matter of course. Very good impact can be gained with monochrome for the bulk of the film, with touches of colour only at key points.

7. A fresh look can sometimes be given to an ordinary subject by using colours out of context, such as black background with figures in white or coloured lines instead of the usual black outline. Grass can be pink and skies green, etc.

8. Subliminal effects can be achieved by putting two close colours like pink and orange on alternate frames. This gives a colour vibration that is not consciously seen, but creates a tension in the viewer. It makes a colour more insistent without it being the brightest colour.

9. Colours are relative in their dominance. In a very brightly-coloured scene, the eye would look for a restful spot, and in a low key scene the eye would focus on the moving or brightest spot. This can be tested by closing your eyes when watching a film, then opening them to see what is the first thing you pick out.

10. Try to build up scenes in colour so that the colour goes with more information, movement, etc. Do not dilute the impact of your key characters by having colours detract from the main line of action.

Look at photos, paintings and still pictures to see how the colour balance leads your eye in or out of the picture. Try to analyse why some pictures are restful to look at and others are not. Look at abstract paintings and see how far a picture can be broken down, yet still retain the feeling for the subject.

Although it is not the writer's job to choose the colours or do the designs, it is the writer's job to make sure that the purpose of the designs is consistent with the storyline.

Give dominant colours to props in use and body parts that identify or move most.

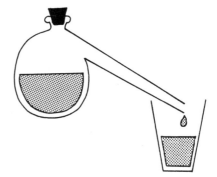

Colour coding to follow through events.

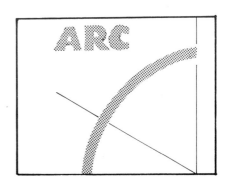

Colour for highlighting significant text or object.

Camera Shots

Animation makes do with three basic shots most of the time as other shots can be created within the artwork.

Long shot (L. S.) is commonly used to establish a scene. In most cases the characters are not recognisable in this field of view. The L. S. is commonly used as the start of a zoom, cut, or pan to create a mood and lead the viewer into the scene. A series of long shots combined with mixes can create a sense of depth as though going through a long tunnel or on an endless road. This shot can also be used to end a scene as if the viewer were moving away.

Mid shot (M. S). Most animation is done with this shot. It shows the characters and the immediate background. It is approximately equal to a stage setting in the theatre. It allows the viewer to see enough of what is going on but keeps the action framed within close limits.

Two shot (T.S.). Very much a development of TV rather than cinema, its use in animation is generally restricted to low budget films where it allows the head and shoulders of two people to be seen as they talk. It limits the animation to the faces and so is used where dialogue is more dominant than movement.

Close up (C. U.) With a character this would be the head and shoulders of one person, but in diagrams it would mean enlarging a particular part of the image to demonstrate a point more clearly. The C. U. has a good dramatic effect if used sparingly, but it is not good to use C. U.'s of faces if they are not well animated.

Large C. U. or Big C. U. (L. C. U. or B. C. U.) This is used totally for dramatic effect. A cut or fast zoom into a character or object will suddenly make the viewer aware of something they were not looking at or giving significance to; it pinpoints the action with great impact. This can also be used in reverse so that a shot starts with a L. C. U. and zooms back to show something unexpected. This deliberate use of ambiguous shots can give interest and new significance to otherwise ordinary objects and situations.

USING THE CAMERA

A. Long shot, mid shot, two shot. B. Close up, big close up, extra big close up. C. High angle shot and ambiguous shot.

The Screen

As a general rule, use of all the screen some of the time, and some of it all of the time, but never all of it all of the time — there are limits to what the eye can stand.

In animation the screen can be thought of as an artist's canvas instead of a stage. You can have characters walking upside down, floating in the air and popping on and off at will. So do not automatically limit yourself to an analogy of the real world.

The screen does put some limits on you, though. These are the practical ones of size. It is obvious that the large cinema screen can show far more detail than that on a TV set. But other factors come into it as well. Animation on TV is likely to be a short advertising commercial, or a filler between programmes, so that the time, place and conditions of viewing are not comparable with the cinema at all, and would suffer if this were not taken into consideration at the design stage.

The small screen requires a different proportion for the characters. The heads, hands, eyes and significant props need to be much larger than for the cinema screen. The backgrounds need to be simpler and the shots mainly from M. S. to C. U. It is also a good idea to stage the characters so that they relate directly to the audience in a way consistent with normal TV staging. Considering how short most films are for TV, it is useful to make more of sound effects than one would for a large screen.

The large screen. With this, people have come to look at the film, and not see it incidentally between other shows. A lot more detail can be put into large screen films which, in turn, allows them a greater range of design. The audience is in a receptive state of mind so will expect more from a cinema film.

Split and multi-screens

Screens can be divided up into smaller areas, or have other screens added on to them. The split screen is very commonly used for titles where it allows live action inserts to be incorporated with the animation. This can create a mood rather than tell a story. In teaching it is a useful device to have the screen split so that one side has illustrations and the other text where this needs special attention.

The multi-screen usually requires several projectors, so is limited in application. It is possible to have a centre screen with a cine projector and side screen with still projectors. An even better way of using this approach is to have banks of still projectors that can flash up images in fast sequences so that there is an effect of animation.

Many versions of the multi-screen have been tried, varying from three screens to a hemisphere made up of dozens of screens and surrounding the viewer.

72

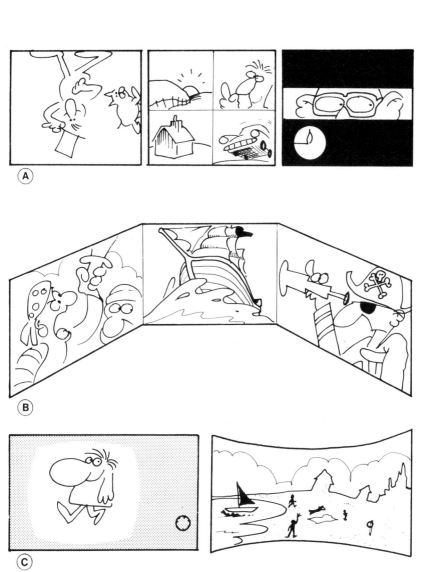

USING THE SCREEN

A. The irrational screen, split screen, masked screen. B. Multi screen. C. Small screen, large figure. Big screen, small figures.

Defining Characters

Most animated films are short, so situations and characters need to be established quickly by the use of clichés. This includes dress, manner, gestures, speech, props and backgrounds. Take a character who is rich; his background will very much determine how this is expressed:
1. *Inherited* riches show someone accustomed to wealth. His manner would show a disdain for money. Dress might be aristocratic, even eccentric.
2. *Earned* riches would show someone who would want to show off their success. Conspicuous consumption in the form of house, car, jewellery might accentuate the power that goes with the affluence.
3. *Won* wealth might show a man unused to handling money. He might dress in expensive but bad taste. His family might do the same. in fact he would use money to extend upon the things he is familiar with rather than use it to change his life-style or gain position.
4. *Stolen* money, like a crook who wants the good life, would show a man spending money lavishly, surrounded by good-time people.
5. *Saved* money. A miser putting his money before human values; dresses badly and acts suspiciously.

Props
Writing out the background of characters is a help to everyone, particularly the designer, and actor, who has to create the voice part. The writing part will include defining the character's own props including: moustaches, beard, haircuts; spectacles, monocles, eye patches; cigarettes and holders, cigars, pipes; jewellery, watches, rings, tiepins, medals and decorations; ceremonial clothes, industrial clothes, national costumes.

Props also include extensions of a character: telephones, musical instruments, umbrellas, weapons, sports equipment, machines, cars, flags, tools, utensils, etc. — anything that allows the user to define a purpose in extension of themselves.

Animation lends itself well to 'magic props' such as wands, magic lamps, wishing wells, flying broomsticks, magic potions, animals and machines with human characteristics, etc., here the prop is used as the medium rather than a direct extension of the character. It must be remembered that magic is an analogy for real power, and is essentially an amplification of something that exists 'Like unto like' so a pumpkin and six mice become a coach and horses. Magic is not creating things out of thin air.

MAKING USE OF CLICHES

A. Cliché characters. B. Props: umbrellas, animals, flags, wands, telephones, alarms, musical instruments, tools and funny clothes.

Animating Words and Symbols

Words often lend themselves to a design consistent with what they describe. There are several ways of doing this: the word might be shaped like the object it describes, such as CAR being shaped like a car. The letters might be designed in a self-descriptive way such as flowery lettering for 'flowers', or blood dripping from the word 'horror'. Dots added to the word 'look': colours added to the word 'rainbow', or the word 'sun' glowing, etc., are typical of ways to make a word stand out as a mnemonic.

It is obvious that such designs lend themselves to animation and so are suitable for setting the mood in film titles and credits, and can even be incorporated into the action of the film. If the styling is consistent then *action words* which are both descriptive of a movement and a sound can add considerable impact to the image; words like Thud! Zonk! Bam! Vrooommmmm!! The use of these words can be found in comics of *Superman* type. With the correct sound effects to go with these words, the action is heightened without interfering with style or content of the film.

The words do not have to describe a violent action; a gloomy character could walk around with the word 'Gloom' above his head, or have 'Think' pop on when he thinks, or 'Bang!!' when he points his finger in a menacing way. In diagrams of what otherwise might be a dull subject, descriptive words can often be given this treatment and make a point come over more strongly. Look at every key word in a script and see if it lends itself to animation and sound effects.

Speech bubbles

We can read much faster than we can speak, so speech bubbles and text can be put on quite fast without interfering with the action. The bubbles themselves can be coloured and shaped consistent with the animation, and key words in the bubbles can be highlighted.

As well as bubbles, characters can be used to bring on words such as titles and credits, or have the titles integrated with the action of the title sequence. Try to think of words as objects that can be used as seats, doors, or anything their shape suggests. Try to make credits and titles work for you by setting the mood and action of the film.

WORDS AS PICTURES

A. Action words. B. Ideograph words. C. Computer animation of typography.

Backgrounds

Backgrounds are very much a matter of fashion. The very full and realistic backgrounds of the early feature films gave way to the stark and abstract backgrounds that followed the break-away from traditional animation.

The purpose of the background is to establish the context and situation. If it is a street scene then this can be reinforced by traffic noises. If it is in the home then radio or TV noise can establish the scene without detailed drawings.

It does not matter how much detail is in the background as long as it does not conflict with the foreground animation. If the background needs full animation, then this should be done as an establishing shot, and limited in length.

Heavily detailed buildings can make a character look small or flat by comparison. Moving vehicles in the background can draw the viewer's attention in the wrong direction. Photographic and pop-art backgrounds have to be used in a constructive way to blend with the overall style otherwise it looks like an animated magazine.

Backgrounds can be implied with textures and colours, and the addition of suitable sound effects, eg: the sound footsteps will make indicate whether the character is inside or outside a building.

Backgrounds can also be popped on and off as required if it is necessary to keep the character on the screen all the time. Generally speaking, the less background you can get away with the more imaginative you can be with the foreground, and as animation is a conceptual medium it should not contain more than is needed.

Live action with animation
Advertising sequences often require a live-action figure over an animated background, or an animated figure over a live-action background. In this case the background should be considered as decorative rather like a stage setting or backdrop. To get animation and live-action to work together convincingly you must work out a balanced styling and consistent movements. this means exaggerating the live-action and toning down the animated movements.

Invisible backgrounds
With the right sound effect, you can use a character to mime the situation. This can be made very effectively by putting in 'sympathy' movements, eg: if an invisible car shoots past, the noise is clear and the rush of air would drag on the character.

As a general rule, leave thinking about backgrounds until the storyline has been worked out and the characters defined. The background should be complementary to these, and should be given as much thought as the characters themselves.

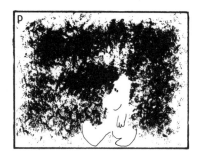

THINKING OF BACKGROUNDS

A. Full background. B. Simplified background. C. Stylised background. D. Textured background. E. Abstract background. F. Implied background (using sound).

79

Animating Technical Diagrams

A very common mistake is to see a diagram in a book used for research, and assume that the diagram simply has to be transferred to the screen and animated. Book diagrams work because they illustrate text that can be referred back to. Also, such diagrams may be studied at leisure, and are often related to other diagrams not on the same page.

Film diagrams have to be totally self-evident if they are to work. They must not have extraneous detail; use words difficult to read (compound technical words) unless these words are themselves highlighted and explained, nor be dependent upon explanations yet to come, or details glossed over earlier in the film.

If text has to be put over a diagram, it is better to put it on at the relevant time, and take if off when it has fulfilled its purpose, so that the screen is never cluttered up. If you need a lot of text, then it may be better to separate this from the diagram and have it written on one side of the screen, or in a scene by itself. If the text is being read while being displayed, do not have the diagram animating as well.

If you are teaching a concept that the audience is not familiar with, use the simplest words and diagrams possible until the concept is clear. Then transfer it to the context of the subject you are dealing with.

So that the audience does not get lost, show a diagram working fully without text or voice. Then add the key information, and simplify the diagram. Having gone through all the details, then show the full working diagram as a summing up of the statement.

Verbal and visual logic

If you are teaching with a blackboard you would present an idea verbally and illustrate the points needing better description. On the other hand, if you had all the illustrations ready, you would put these up and present the ideas visually, only going into detailed verbal explanations when the illustrations were not self-evident.

Every shape has a sound

Diagrams can be boring to watch if the viewer has to work out what they mean. Isolate the meaningful information of each frame and give this a sound. An example would be to show the curve of a graph going up with an accompanying sound, and a 'Ping!' at key points. Moving parts of a diagram might be given a tune that comes on every time the part works. Use sound to isolate and focus images that otherwise have little in design or movement working for them.

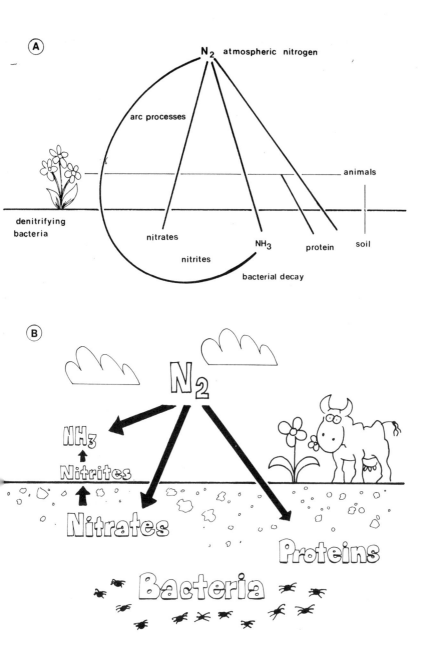

ANIMATING BOOK DIAGRAMS

The nitrogen cycle. A. Book diagram. B. Film version. The book version allows a reference to the text but the film version must immediately present significant information.

The Soundtrack

There are three separate sources for a soundtrack — the voice track, the music track, and effects track. An audience hears sound in this order: effects, music, voice. The first is immediately associated with the visual (and even anticipated), the second has a mood or rhythm consistent with action, and the third requires reflection upon.

Sound effects

Animation rarely uses real effects unaltered. To match the visual, the sound must be exaggerated in some way and given more of its distinguishing characteristic. This can be done on real effects by changing the speed, giving it echo, superimposing two sounds, cutting two sounds together as one, adding or subtracting part of the frequency range, putting the sound through special effects machines such as sound synthesizers, etc.

A typical distortion would have to be a human voice speeded up until it sounds like Donald Duck, or add a musical tone so that it sounds like a talking piano.

Some effects (such as lunar sounds) are created totally by sound synthesizers and have no parallel in reality. Other sound effects are real (such as a gong) but played at a speed that allows them to be used for a different purpose yet still retain the same audience response. Sound and image shapes can be distorted in the same way, and some sounds will even suggest the images.

Try to think up sounds for non-existent things such as a dinosaur's roar, a Genii coming out of a magic lamp, footsteps on the moon, a machine that makes thingamajigs.

Sources of effect

Listen to radio plays and see how much the effects used contribute to your mental images. See if you can pick out sound effects added to films (particularly fast action films like Kung Fu adventures). See what sort of sound effects can be made with ordinary household utensils such as saucepans, knives, and forks, matchboxes, glasses.

It is very common for sound effects to be overlooked in a script, and if just left to the editor with no indication of what is needed, he has the choice of putting on what happens to be available, or having to spend time creating something especially for it. Also, the wrong sound effect does not become evident until the first screening of sound and picture. Quite often the 'wrong' effect conveys a concept more effectively than one that seems more logical.

In animation it is the 'effect' that makes the abstract concrete. Suggestions as to what sounds are needed and how they might be used are part of the script.

Real and simulated effects.

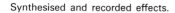

Synthesised and recorded effects.

Instrumental and voice effects.

Music for Animation

A good soundtrack has saved many a dull film, and even the most meaningless abstract squiggles can be made to work with the right music.

At one level, music can be used as a background to create a mood. In this case it simply has to be consistent with the atmosphere of the story. This is done in advertising jingles where a catchy musical phrase identifies the 'mood' of the product.

Music can be used as a sound effect. This is evident in many classical works, eg. La Mer, Peter and the Wolf, Carnival of Animals, etc. In films the music can imitate the actual sound effects it replaces, or the rhythm of movement (trains, traffic, machines, walks, etc.). If music is to be used in this way, then the design of the characters would take this into account, and their walks and gestures should be suited to musical phrasing.

Music as Part of the Film

If the film is about a musician, band, or includes a musical device (radio, TV) then other musical aspects can be brought in. Suppose two neighbors play instruments. One plays bass and the other flute. One disturbs the other by playing too loud, and the other retaliates by playing even louder. The instruments have by analogy become weapons, and this extends to the musical notes being bullets. The bass might use the strings to send missiles. The flute might be used as a peashooter and so on.

Having the source of music controlled by the characters in the film allows numerous effects to be achieved that help define the characters and create the situations.

Music as the basis of the story

Music has a sense of shape, size, texture and direction. If you start with these in mind and try to visualise a piece of music then you will find it suggests ideas — even colours and dances. Visualising sound itself can be helped by studying how sound recordings are made — the patterns on optical soundtracks, oscilloscopes, record tracks, etc. It is also common to use psychedelic patterns in programmes playing pop music, also the sort of visual effects used in clubs where pop music is played indicates the relationship between sound and visuals.

Look at record covers and see how designers visualise the music of the record. Try to sing, whistle, and hum ideas of your own related to the script. And, above all, listen to sounds of things that you take for granted.

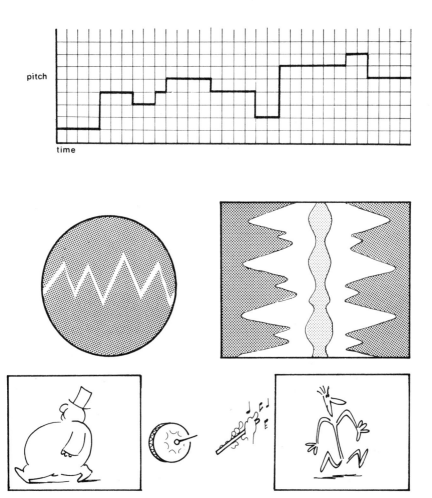

USING MUSIC

A. Music depicted on a graph, plotting pitch against time. B. Oscilloscope trace of musical sounds and the optical soundtrack are visual representations of sound. C. Visual/sound matching. Fat man, heavy slow footsteps matched to a big brass drum. Thin, lithe energetic man matched to a flute.

The Voicetrack

Voice-over (V. O.)

Because animated characters do not actually speak, giving them voices is really a matter of presentation. The majority of animated films do not have voicetracks at all, and it is usually considered an achievement to write a film that does not need a voice. But that is not always possible, so the writer must consider what contribution the voice will make, and how to use it.

The simplest way to use a voice is as an off-screen narration telling the story as it is animated. This is fine for technical and educational films as these may not have characters in them. For children's films that have characters, the voice-over can be a different voice for each figure. The lips do not move or, at most, will do so in a rudimentary way on the figures, which will convey their intent by postures and gestures.

The next stage up from this is cut-outs or puppets that have a few basic lip shapes. These are not strictly synchronised, but simply show who happens to be talking at the time.

Lip synchronisation

Making characters talk with the correct lip shapes requires very skilful animating and editing, and is very expensive. Few films besides features and advertising commercials go this far.

Apart from the actual expense involved initially, it also creates problems for dubbing in foreign languages. To some extent the amount of work and costs can be cut down by using tricks that appear to give lip sync but disguise the lips by using cigarettes, pipes, beards and moustaches, big noses, high collars, and hands appropriately placed. Popeye is a good example of using the pipe; Bugs Bunny often speaks while eating carrots. By making the right gestures and expressions, accurate lip sync can be reduced or avoided ... with a significant cut in work.

Where lip sync is used, it is necessary to keep the phrases short and simple — subtlety does not work too well in animation. The voices have also to be exaggerated when recorded. This should be mentioned in the script or told to the actors before recording,

The effect of voices can be augmented to at the recording by adding echo, changing the pitch, squashing and stretching, etc. Try to have the voices of characters clear in your mind before recording, and if you are present at the recording, read the storyboard as it's being recorded to check that the timing is right for all the action otherwise all the effort going into lip sync will be wasted if it competes with other movements.

USING VOICES

A. Lip-sync. B. Limited lip-sync. Use of props can reduce the amount of animation of the lips. C. Body poses and expressions can convey speech more effectively than lips alone.

Rehearsing an animated film.

The Line Test

When an animator wants to check a difficult piece of animation, or to match it up accurately with a soundtrack, he can do a line test, which is usually a pencil drawing (line without colour) version of the scene. This is shot in monochrome and processed quickly, as a check.

The beauty of the line test is that only the part to be checked need be drawn accurately, not the backgrounds or incidental animation. It can also be shot on 16mm, even if the final version is to be shot on 35mm.

The line test can be edited and synchronised to the soundtrack and cut into the final version with the finished shots. It is then replaced as the final version of each scene is ready.

In a feature film it is sometimes useful to have a final version of a character in full colour shot with a line test of other characters to see how they work together. All animators do test films for themselves and it is worth discussing ideas with them and doing tests if you have an idea that you are not sure of.

Moving storyboard

Sometimes clients find it difficult to visualise a storyboard working, especially if the soundtrack plays an important part. This can be overcome by drawing up a neat version of the storyboard in full colour and shooting this with key artwork synchronised with the track. It will not contain any animation, but camera movements can be included to give a sense of action. This storyboard can be shot on to film, with a separate soundtrack, or it can be shot as slides and run with a tape recording of the soundtrack.

Pilot film

When a series is going into production, or even a special once-only film, then a pilot would probably be made. This would be in every way a final version of the film but used to assess the film from various viewpoints. It may never be shown publicly, but still meet the specifications of being timed, costed, and marketed as for rest of the series. The pilot may be done in two or three versions with different presenters, voices, or even treatments. The writer is expected to draft out the various possibilities. A hidden trap is that it is sometimes possible to come up with a brilliant pilot idea, but when given the go-ahead, find a series of comparable ideas do not come so easily. In a situation like this the writer should be quite clear on what basis the idea works, and have a few similar ideas drafted out that can be followed up. The problem of 'drying up' with ideas happens to everyone. Do not put everything into a pilot just to sell it and then leave yourself an even bigger problem.

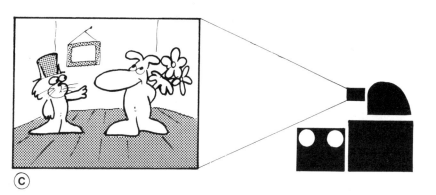

REHEARSING ANIMATING

A. The line test made in black and white for the animator. B. The final frame as it would appear in the film. C. The 'moving storyboard' referred to as an Animatic or Leica reel. Made for the client in colour.

Animation Stand (Rostrum Camera)

The writer should be familiar with the range and limitations of the camera in the studio as, to some extent, these affect the styling and quality of work the studio produces. Special effects lenses, ultra-violet lighting, back projection, aerial image, rotoscoping, and the like are typical extras above the normal and basic operations of the stand. Some stands are computer operated, others adapted to shoot at live-action speeds when only camera movements are required (no change in artwork).

There is a growing trend for animators to work 'under the camera' — which means improvising. In effect, this means having only a loose script to work from. A storyboard would have the key scenes in with accurate timings. This type of animation will have a voice track added *after* the animation.

Editing machine
However well-defined and timed the script is, there will always be different interpretations, variations and mistakes at the recordings, that necessitate doing a number of 'takes' of the script. The editor has to juggle these about to fit the image. But the image track will also have scenes shot to a greater length than necessary with possible variations on transitions. This allows the soundtrack to be shifted in relation to the image and also for sound effects to be cut in without overriding the voice. The editing machine allows both sound and image tracks to be run together and be matched up on the correct frames. The writer often has to advise at this stage on what interpretation is intended.

Synchroniser
This is used by the editor to do the soundtrack breakdown. In principle it is similar to the editing machine, but is hand-operated. The editor runs the soundtrack back and forth on a sprocketed wheel attached to a frame counter. A recording head plays the sound as the editor checks the frame numbers for the start and end of the sound. This gives him the actual length in frames for each sound and its place in the track as a whole. This information is transferred to a 'dope sheet' against which the animator can match the drawings.

Dope sheet (camera sheet)
In effect, the dope sheet is the shooting version of the storyboard. The editor puts the soundtrack breakdown on it and gives it to the animator who codes the drawings to match the track. The animator writes in the relevant camera movements beside the drawings, and when the drawings for a scene have been finished these, and the dope sheet, go to the cameraman.

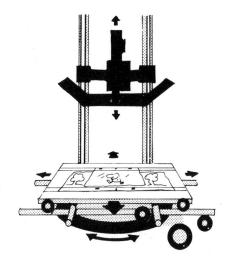

The animation stand (rostrum). The camera can move up and down the column (zooming). The table can move sideways north, south, east and west and rotate.

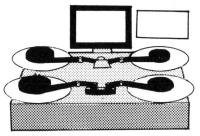

The editing machine. Allows convenient juxtaposition of picture and sound.

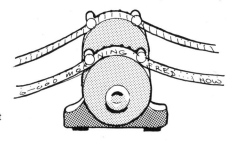

The synchroniser. Allows convenient 'marking up' of soundtracks.

91

Stopwatch and Tape

It is not unknown for a five minute script to be ten minutes long when recorded! The most useful talent the scriptwriter can develop is a sense of how long it takes to say and do something. It requires the timing of every phrase, movement and scene until it works 'naturally' in the allotted time.

If you are timing a character doing something that can be acted out, then you should act it out yourself while holding the stopwatch. only check the stopwatch at the end of the movement. Do not speed up the movements to beat the watch but rewrite the part so that it works at the right speed.

If the animation cannot be acted out directly, such as an explosion, or an engine working, then use your hands to trace out the movement in the air. If someone is available to time you, go over a movement a number of times to get an average of the timings.

If you do not have a stopwatch handy, you can time a movement by tracing a circle in the air and counting 'A thousand and one, a thousand and two . . .' Do this with a watch to get the rhythm in your mind. Once this has been established you will not need a watch for movements of a few seconds. If you count with your eyes closed to imagine the animation, then a movement taking $1\frac{1}{2}$ seconds will mean you have traced $1\frac{1}{2}$ circles in the air. Such timings can be critical on TV commercials where every second costs money.

Tape recorder

The aural storyboard is the best way to get timing accurate. Record the script while looking at the storyboard and allowing for movements and transitions. Make sure you keep a steady rhythm for each scene. You can also put some of the effects in as you are going; these are only indicators and not meant to be accurate.

Once you have recorded the script, play it back and act out the whole thing, mentally noting how consistent this is with how you imagine it should be. It is a common mistake to record too fast on each phrase and not leave enough time between phrases.

It is even better if you can record the script while someone else is acting it out. Go over it again, even altering the storyboard to fit the actions. If you get the whole thing working in your mind then you find that the technical problems sort themselves out much more easily, as you will know the effect you will want to achieve.

TIMING THE STORYBOARD

Record the script while looking at the storyboard.

Play back the recording and act out the storyboard and note where the timing is wrong.

Time critical movements by acting them out while holding a stopwatch.

A picture is worth a thousand copies.

Copying Machine

You cannot use a copying machine too much. Get copies of your script and storyboard as soon as possible and get fresh copies of every new draft. Do not work with overwritten, tattered, coffee-stained scripts, or suffer the inconvenience of losing the only copy. Also, make sure that copies go to *everyone* who has comments to make on the script or needs to refer to it. This includes the client, producer, director, designer, animator and editor. And get the secretary to file spare copies; the actors will need them later — and *before* they get to the recording studio.

Grant projector (Lucy)
There are various types and names for this form of projector which allows pictures to be shown on a frosted glass screen and traced off. This is useful if you find illustrations during script research that are needed for the storyboard. They may be the wrong size, or contain too much irrelevant detail. You can trace off what you need at the right scale, and even run off copies of this if the drawing is part of a cycle.

Rotoscope
Apart from its use in combining live-action with animation (see page 78) it can also be used with microfilm to project technical drawings on to photosensitive copying paper to get hard-copy artwork that can be painted.

Very good textural effects can be achieved by projecting an image on to paper that is laid on top of textured material such as wood, or fine metal gratings. Rubbing a coloured pencil over the defined area will produce a pattern without the hard outline. This can be done in different colours with varying textures changing through the scene.

Lightbox
The animator's drawing board is basically a sheet of glass with a light behind it. A drawing put on the light box will show through a clean sheet of paper laid on top and allow the animator to trace over it and make the next stage of movement. The skilled animator can put several levels of drawings on top of each other, and flip through them to see the animation moving.

If the writer works closely with the animator, suggestions can be made to get the right sort of movement in detailed gestures.

The more the writer understands of these techniques, the more the script will exploit what can be done easily and well by the production team. It is only by constantly discussing ideas at every stage that suggestions for achieving the desired ends will be put forward, otherwise the script will tend to 'escape' from the writer in subtle ways not easy to recognise.

STORYBOARD AIDS

A. A copying machine can be of great help when preparing storyboards. A basic picture can be modified to show a sequence of events. B. The Grant projector allows reduction and enlargement of material and relevant parts traced off. C. Rotoscoping. Using the rostrum camera as a projector live-action film can be traced to allow matching to animation.

How Far Can An Image be Processed?

The animator's original drawings can be added to considerably by optical effects within the camera. This film again can be changed by further superimposing, optical printing, etc. But even when everything that can be done in the studio *has* been done, there are still processes that change the image even more.

Film labs
Without actually changing the picture, the way it is processed in the labs can give a range of interesting effects.

One effect, often seen on film titles, is to have the film processed to high contrast so that only the dark shadows show. This gives the live-action image a hard edge and block colouring similar to that used in animation and matches well with it. The film can then be optically coloured to extend the effect further. A surrealistic effect can be achieved by having a colour reversal print, which shows all the colours as their opposites and, perhaps, cutting this in with a normal positive.

Model animation used in live-action films needs to have trick effects in scaling (giants walking through cities), or double exposures (people talking to themselves as identical twins). These effects are done in the labs, using techniques such as travelling mattes that black out one part of the film while it is being shot, and then film another picture on to the blacked-out part.

Some interesting psychedelic effects can be achieved by processing to give uneven texture or development. Films can also be tinted to give them a 'period' look.

Video studio
Many of the above effects can be achieved electronically if the film has been transferred to videotape. By using chromakey colours for the lettering and blocked areas of animation these areas do not show the actual colour, but the film that is being superimposed. This allows a live-action film to appear as the animated shapes.

If two tapes are made of the same film, they can be combined out of phase to give trailing images of the same picture. These can be used with a colour synthesiser to make a whole range of constantly-changing colours and effects.

If a film is made specially for TV such as a commercial, or TV insert, then there are many advantages to writing in TV effects and having the animation coloured and styled for this type of processing. As there is continual technological advance in electronic image processing, the writer should be familiar with the range of facilities that video offers to animation.

96

USING THE LABS

A. Processing an image to high contrast tones and edge generation. B. Alternate frames of positive and negative images with drop-shadow version creates a strong visual impact. C. Combining model animation and live action footage using back--projection. The labs will do many tests to get the colour balance correct.

Photographic Studio

Photo-animation is a technique commonly used to save drawing time. Photographs are used as a basis for the artwork, and the figures may be cut-outs of photos. There are, however, many still photography techniques that are not available for movies.

If an animated film is to be made about a well-known person (for good or for bad), existing photographs from magazines and papers can be used, or the person can pose for a series of shots to cover the various movement cycles needed. These can be made humorous by putting the head of one person on the body of another or combining pictures out of scale so the body, for example, might have very large feet and head.

Front projection

Some photographic studios are equipped with front projection facilities. This set up enables a foreground object or person to be combined realistically with a projected background image. The image is projected along the camera lens axis on to a special high-reflectance screen behind the subject.

Because of its special surface, only the screen and not the person reflects this image back to the camera, and the person may even be lit separately without affecting the background. Thus he is realistically combined with his (projected) background image.

Computer animation

It is common for scientists, engineers, architects, and those producing technical drawings to have these made into films by computer techniques. These films have very limited styling, being primarily concerned with the information content. But they often need a script and the addition of a soundtrack and colour to emphasise key points.

The most usual output of computers in this field is microfilm, some giving colour, but most black and white. The monochrome forms can be coloured optically or transferred to videotape and coloured electronically.

If the artwork needs to be integrated with photographs or normal animation then the computer can be used to actually draw the images on to paper or cel by using one of the various types of plotter available. The best use of computer animation is where the information canot be created in any other way such as in technical subjects. However, the lack of individuality in this form tends to make it hard on the eye after a short while, so this should be considered at the script stage.

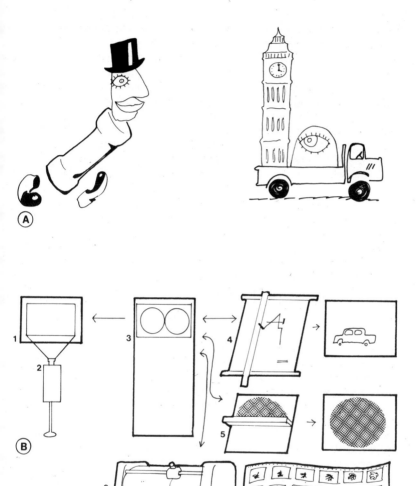

SPECIAL TECHNIQUES

A. Composite pictures made from photo cut-outs. B. Computer animation. 1. cathode ray tube. 2. camera. 3. computer. 4. flat-bed plotter producing line drawings. 5. matrix plotter producing half tone drawings. 6. drum plotter producing drawings in batch form.

People in the Studio

Responsibility for delivering the finished film to the client on time, at the agreed cost, and to the client's satisfaction lies with the producer.

Producer

The producer has to assign personnel and facilities to the job, set the deadlines and budget each stage. To do this the script has to contain enough information for realistic estimates.

As estimates cannot be made without some sort of script and as having a script means, to some extent, working on the production, it is common for a producer to book the scriptwriter to do an outline or exploratory script which suggests ideas and approaches. The client's comments on this then form a basis for production estimates.

Estimating time and cost

The producer may have experience in similar films, but every film has unique problems, so *hidden* costs can be the producer's nightmare. Such costs might come about with special effects, copyright material or live-action clips, that are written into the script but not detailed. These might easily be passed over at the script stage, and not come to light until the production is under way. It is the scriptwriter's job to work closely with the producer at the early stages and make sure that all the points in the script are clear and accountable within the studio's range of expertise and facilities.

A good producer should make an effort to understand the script and offer constructive criticism so that technical and production problems are eliminated at this stage without detracting from the creative aspect. A good producer should also include the writer in all client meetings and the early production meetings, where these affect the script. He should also set up screenings of similar films where these might help the writer.

A bad producer may offer little information at any level, exlcuding the writer from client and production meetings, and making insignificant changes in the script (while often taking a script credit), and calling in other people to make script changes without notifying the writer. He may often talk in terms of 'deals' rather than the film in hand, and stand to gain financially (rather than in reputation) from the film being made. On any film, make sure you establish a good working relationship with the producer and are quite clear as to what is expected from each of you.

Client **Producer**

Budget
costing
creative
administrative
overheads
contingencies
stock
processing

Studio Personnel
writer
director
designers
animators
editor
cameraman
painters
actors
musicians
consultants

Schedule
deadlines
storyboard
designs
production
line tests
viewing copy
final print

Facilities
allocation
cameras
editing equipment
threatres
dubbing
labs

101

Director

The conception of the final film is the job of the director. It means getting an overall consistency in story, design, soundtrack and style of animation. Often the director is also the designer or animator (even editor).

When the written script is ready to go into a storyboard the director is called in to discuss the way this is to be treated — decisions determined by budget, time, available personnel/facilities, market and so on. It is the director's style that finally makes the film what it is, and this style is based upon his or her attitude to life and reference points. Getting to know how a director sees and feels about things is very much a part of the writer's job, otherwise the interpretation of his script may be far removed from his intentions.

The director has to know the background of the script — where the research was done, and what other sources were used, what other films have been made on the subject, and how these treated it (eg: what market or age level they were aimed at). The director must make sure the storyboard flows smoothly so that there are no abrupt cuts or jumps from one scene to another and also check that the timing is right for the action needed. The writer must be able to justify the approach taken in the script, and offer alternatives if technical or creative problems prevent the director from achieving the consistency required.

The common problem where characters 'get away' from their creators (especially in animation where a minor character may be styled and animated in a way that it upstages the key characters) and other possible interpretations must be resolved by discussion between the director and writer. These may continue right through the film.

Recording
When the storyboard is finished, the next stage of production is the recording. The director is in charge of the recording but the writer should be present in case the script needs rewriting either for length or phrasing — also to advise on interpretation. At this point the writer has finished the script, but changes in the script can go on right through the film as new ideas occur, or certain scenes do not work as expected, and need rewriting. It makes the director's job a lot easier if the writer has given copies of the script to all concerned, and familiarized them with the ideas involved. The director must also discuss this in detail with everyone and be responsible for having it done.

MATCHING TALENT, TIME AND MONEY

The director.

Designer

The design is all-important. Imagine Mickey Mouse and Donald Duck as any other mouse or duck. The design has several endpoints to satisfy. It must be consistent with the script, it must be consistent with the rest of the characters and backgrounds, it must animate easily, and must somehow sum up the film and become a mnemonic for it.

A well-designed character becomes more famous than any film star, and has spin-off in too many directions to mention. But the majority of animated films do not aim this high, and are successful if the characters work sufficiently well to tell the story over.

The designer works with the writer to get the feeling for the characters — how they walk, what they wear, gestures and mannerisms, props and habits. Quite often designs are done at the ideas stage and the story developed around the designs (common practice in short films and TV commercials).

A common mistake with clients is to take an existing design from a comic strip, advertising character, etc. and assume that because it works in one medium it will transfer to another. It rarely does without some design amendments. The problems become worse if an established character, say from a newspaper strip has to be given a voice, which of course, has not been established with the strip. The designer has to retain the feeling for the character, yet style it so the movements seem natural — giving it weight and volume that are not evident in a still character.

Similar problems arise when animals without hands (birds, hoofed animals, even snakes, etc.) are required to manipulate things. This can be done without question in still pictures, but imagine an elephant trying to put on a bow tie! The writer has to bear in mind the sort of problems the designer has to face when working in animation where the whole universe has to be reconceived.

Design problems can be very expensive if not solved at the storyboard stage. Every extra piece of clothing means another colour to be painted on the cel. A striped suit takes twice as long to animate as a plain suit. A flowing gown can be a nightmare to animators, and furry animals with all the hairs showing will not make you popular with anyone if they are included in the script.

The script and storyboard should be accompanied by any illustrations, references, photographs and suggestions that help in arriving at the final designs.

no eyeballts just use dots

small tuft of hair between ears

keep ears springy

Hilite on nose

three whiskers

keep arms springy like ears

belly button

no toes on feet

stance sticks belly out and shoulders back

CREATING CHARACTER

A. The model sheet. B. The same character in different costume can considerably increase the animators work. C. Wings, hooves, and paws etc. can take on the expressions of hands.

Animator

The layman often believes that animated films are produced entirely by the animator, and that scripts, designs, and camera effects, etc., are all inherent in the drawing. This is not the case; the animator is a special type of artist whose art is closer to acting than drawing.

Good animators are good mimics. They can imitate voices and actions, and have a sense of timing that goes with acting. Oddly enough, many of them are not good artists graphically, but this is not always essential. Like all artists, they have subjects that interest them more than others. Some like animating technical objects like cars, machines, and the like. Others are good at caricatures or special effects, etc.

The writer should become well acquainted with the animator's subjects and styles, and write to exploit these aspects of their work.

Background artist

A background artist is often a painter who spends a great deal of time over a single drawing (as against the thousands the animator does). Their work goes into much greater detail and, in particular, the creation of effects and textures.

Typographer

The typographer's special knowledge of lettering and abstract design is constantly used for film credits, titles and logos in advertising. Imaginative use of lettering can set up the atmosphere of the film before it starts. Its use in a humorous way can add impact to otherwise static scenes.

Cartoonist

The cartoonist is usually a good ideas-man, and often draws up storyboards. His strong points include having well-defined characters – often worked out over a period of years – and the ability to create situations that highlight these characters. His weak point is usually that he may lack film-sense and does not use the idea of movement or sound to reinforce the situation. Many good films have come from collaborations with established cartoonists and film writers or animators.

Draughtsmen and architects

Technical animation is a fast growing field, and more artists with technical backgrounds are taking up animation. Apart from the subjects related to their training, such artists can often work out complex animation movements, and perspective viewpoints where 3D animation is involved.

MAKING A CHARACTER LIVE

A. The animator is responsible for preparing the drawings that represent all the phases of movement that the character is required to go through. B. The background artist must be capable of creating many moods and working in different styles. C. Technical artists specialise in animating technical diagrams and architectural drawings.

The Cameraman

When the animation drawings have been completed, they are checked and taken to the cameraman with the dopesheet (see page 90). The camera instruction, put in by the animator, are in most cases routines. But sometimes the animator may want an effect that he thinks the camera can produce if used in another way. For example, he might want to fade the image to black, while various parts are still moving, and have some parts of the image fade-off before others. This requires combinations of masking, fading, and superimposing, while still retaining the right light level for the whole image. The cameraman would be able to devise tests for such a shot, and perhaps even suggest other methods of doing it to get the same effect.

Such a complex transition could be very effective, but in the storyboard it might only be written 'Fade to black'. The director or animator might take it upon himself to put in the complex fade, but the writer (who should have put it in) and the cameraman (who will do it) in most cases, will not have discussed it. It is a good idea for the writer to talk to the cameraman about such ideas, as he may well have done such an effect for a previous film, or tests of a similar kind. Also, to ask the cameraman what type of effects can be done on the camera they are using (special lens, aerial image, back projection, etc).

Cameramen are often ex-animators, so go over the storyboard with them and see if they can suggest ideas for shots that might be written in to the script.

The Editor
Even after the film is shot, there are still ways to improve the animation by adept cutting, and shifting the soundtrack around. In fact the editor is the 'Mr Fixit' of the studio. His knowledge is particularly useful in finding odd clips of film and soundtracks that have been made for other films but not used.

It is common practice to shoot transitions and cycles longer than necessary so that the soundtrack can be juggled around. Also to have several variations of the soundtrack so that it can be cut to fit the image. These can be 'rough cut' together and run on separate tracks of the editing machine to get an idea of how they match up. The editor works with the storyboard and dopesheet, but it is his sense of timing that makes the combined sound and image work - or not.

It is an advantage if the writer can go through the rough-cut version with the editor to see how the emphasis can be changed from one image to another by the placing of the soundtrack. Getting a feeling for this helps in writing in emphasis words and effects and matching them in the storyboard.

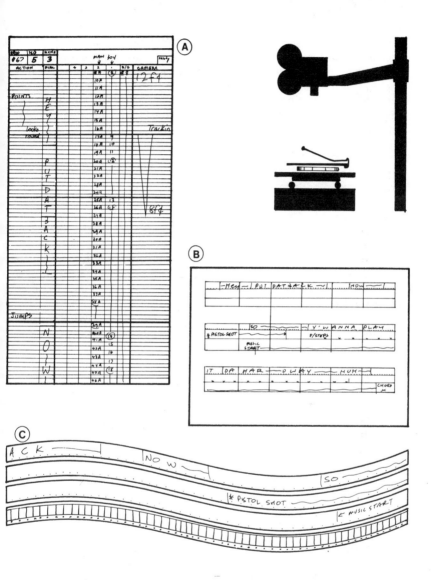

PUTTING SOUND TO VISUAL

A. The dope sheet. This is made out by the animator and contains all the information the cameraman needs to shoot the scene. B. The bar sheet. This is made out by the editor and gives all the details of timings to enable the animator to work. C. When the film has been shot the editor should be able to match the picture, with very little alteration, to the soundtracks.

109

People Out of the Studio

The client is the person who pays for the film. As the majority of animated films are sponsored there is nearly always a client to deal with, although the writer is not always involved at this stage (but should be). Clients are often surprised that animation is very expensive, takes a long time to produce, and does not always look like Walt Disney's work. They are often surprised that thirty minutes of notes and suggestions will not turn into a ten minute film. In spite of this, clients do know what they want when they see it.

Questions for the client
The sort of questions to ask the client are:

Who is going to see the film? What do you want them to think after having seen it? Where are they going to see it? About how long should the film be? How often will it be seen? What is the life expectancy of the film? What other films or material will go with it?

Try to isolate three key points that have to be put over, and then discuss these in order of merit. Have a list of questions ready, and leave questions to be thought about later if they are relevant but have not been considered by the client.

Do not take a brief from the client if you are not sure what is needed. Get him to underline the main points of the brief and detail these, going over them repeatedly until it is absolutely clear that you are both talking about the same things.

It is very common for a brief to get changed several times before going into production, and this is nearly always on account of basic ideas not being clear at the brief stage.

Ask the client what he has seen that he likes and does not like, and ask what other aproaches he has thought about and why these may have been rejected (you may save going over ground already covered). Suggest approaches if they occur to you at the time, but do not push any idea until you have had long enough to think about it.

If you are dealing with a committee of clients, all of whom have a need to make their point, it is worth keeping your own rejected ideas so that they may reject them themselves – leaving you better ideas to be judged on their merits.

Clients sometimes produce rough scripts of their own, and half expect your job to be one of tidying up. Make quite sure you know who is responsible for the final version before you start on such arrangements.

THINKING OF THE AUDIENCE

A. Who sees it? Is the audience specialist or general? B. What should they remember and how often will it be seen? C. Where will it be seen? In the home, the cinema or the club? D. Is it linked with books, talks, advertising or a series? E. How long will it be and how long will it last?

111

The Agent

An agent is someone who acts on behalf of the client. He or she may have worked in the film or TV industry at some stage, or at least have a good knowledge of who does what, where, and for how much. It is the agent's task to advise the client on drawing up a brief for the job, so it is unlikely that the writer, or even producer, will meet the actual client.

If the agent is from an advertising agency, their designers and copywriter will have drawn up scripts and storyboards as guides. In this case the writer is expected to produce a shooting script, or other ideas along the same lines. Sometimes the agency is not sure whether animation is the answer to their problem, and may approach the studio with an open brief to work out some ideas. For this, the writer must produce at least three variations, or even totally different approaches to the problem, plus a 'rationale' — a summary stating why such approaches should be effective. This is a safeguard against whimsical writers who are out to indulge their fantasies at the expense of the agency. It is reasonably certain that the agency will have approached other studios with the same brief.

Freelance agent
A freelance agent/producer could be anyone who has a client with a job. Here, the agent works on a fee basis to collect the various people together and get the job done. He usually works with people he knows well. But there can be the problem that if he is only paid on the condition of getting the right ideas first (selling the idea to the client) then the work offer becomes speculative, and a writer might find himself turning out ideas for little or no return. The way to avoid this is to agree on a rejection fee — being $\frac{1}{4}$-$\frac{1}{2}$ the agreed fee for the accepted job. Make sure the fee is agreed before you start (get it in writing if possible), and keep copies of all you do.

The other writer
Freelance jobs often come in via other writers, or where more than one writer has been approached to do the same job. This can lead to difficulties if it is not clearly defined who is doing what.

If you are to collaborate with another writer, then it is a good start for both to write out a total idea, and then to choose one, rather than have a confusion of styles and approaches all the way through. It is also better to have one person to do the final version, in which case the other will be more useful in doing a thorough research or background development.

Writers tend to be good at *either* strong plot, *or* good dialogue and characterisation. Exploit your own strength in collaboration rather than in competition.

112

ON BEHALF OF THE CLIENT

A. The company agent. He usually works for a large company that has a creative group within it. He would also go to several studios for treatments on the same idea.
B. The freelance agent. He works in association with several companies and is in touch with a large number of creative and technical people. He will tend to work with the same studios for most of the work.

The Consultant

Films on specialised subjects usually have a consultant. His or her job is to be around when advice is needed, and check the script at each stage. At worst, this can be someone who believes he is actually writing the script or insists that, in reality, atoms are not 'green, round, and make a 'boing' sound when they bump into things'. At best, they are (mostly) experts in their field who see that no technical mistakes are made.

Problems often arise when there is no visual analogy for a concept (what does a black hole in the universe look like?), or where the concept may be described in acceptable but contradictory ways, e.g: light might be considered as waves in one analogy, and particles in another. Some mathematical ideas can be described at one level but not another eg: x, x^2, x^3 can be shown as dimensions of space, but x^9 cannot be described visually as an extension of these. Translating ideas from a literal or symbolic notation to a visual one is both difficult in finding the right image, and in convincing the expert that the concept is still being protrayed accurately, if they have not worked in films before.

It is the writer's job to produce a film that is cinematically acceptable. A dull, boring, accurate film has nothing to offer anyone. On the other hand a film that 'bends' the facts within the bounds of poetic licence in order to keep it lively and memorable, will achieve its ends. When working with the consultant, ask if the subject does have any quirks, oddities or aspects that lend themselves to a humorous or visual treatment. These can often be based upon common misconceptions about a subject, eg: that computers can think or perform superhuman tasks, when in fact they are little more than sophisticated tools.

Do not go over every detail at first, but get the three or four key facts down, clear in your mind, and visualised in some form. Then work out the details from there. When writing the script, get the first version down for *content* – saying the correct things, after which the developments can concentrate on *style* – saying them in a memorable way.

Do not bother the consultant about everything if it can be easily checked by yourself, otherwise you will spend a lot of time defining things that are not much use to the film. Try to work out as much as possible yourself, and check up when it does not make sense.

It is always a good idea to tell the consultant that he will be getting a credit as 'Technical Advisor' on the film. This will make him more enthusiastic, and prevents him from asking for a script credit.

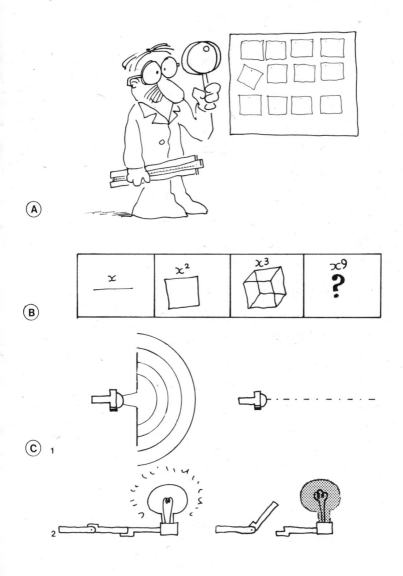

BEING RIGHT AND LOOKING RIGHT

A. The consultant. B. Crystalise key facts. C. Visualising to suit the point being made.
(1) light as waves and light as particles. (2) using a mechanical analogy to convey the
intangible idea of a logic gate in a computer.

The Actors

Animation uses actors who specialise in *voices* as opposed to the actors of stage and screen. To do voices for animation means being able to create standard accents and phrasing that immediately identifies the character, and are consistent with the visual portrayal.

The demand upon the actors can be considerable if they are given little to work from, for example, a script without a storyboard received just prior to the recording. It becomes nearly impossible to do a good job if the actor has to do several voices in one film — a demand common in animation.

The sort of information the actor needs to create a voice includes:

Age of character

State of health: Bouncy, vital and sharp, or slow and cautious.

State of mind: Bright and articulate or dull and stupid.

Situation: Plenty of action requiring quick phrasing, or passive and thoughtful with considered remarks.

Surroundings: Do the characters speak loud, as outside, or soft, as inside?

Age of audience: For children, with the emphasis on key words, or for adults, with subtle intonations?

Speech impediments: Stutters, lisps, grunts, squeaks, um's and er's of hesitant phrasing.

Character actions: The characters may sometimes make elaborate gestures which reinforce their speech.

Rank: If one character is speaking down to another, the tones of condescension must be heard.

Geography: Accents and intonations. Dialects and jargon.

A summary of the characters and their attitudes enables actors to get into the skin of them, otherwise they can lose the 'feel' of the character half way through a script. Apart from the summary, the writer or director should have supplied the script some days at least, before the recording. Actors must also be given time enough at the recording to run through the script, making the appropriate gestures to help them get the feeling for the part. This cannot be done when they are sitting in the recording booth.

When there are several actors, make sure each one has a script with their own parts clearly marked, and also the key words marked with notes on pauses, etc. If an actor finds a passage difficult to say or phrase, let him rephrase it in his own way. Ask the actors to suggest variations on voices, particularly funny ones. If parts of the script have to be recorded again because of mistakes, go over the whole phrase and not just the incorrect words as these can sound wrong out of context. Also, keep a check on timing as it is being read.

As a general rule, the actors should get enough time to know the part, but should not have to rehearse it to the point where they become stale in the delivery.

116

INTERPRETING THE VOICES

The actor. The character he is asked to play must be defined before he can begin. Is the character stupid or smart, young or old, active or passive? What class is he, what accent should he have and what social role does he play?

The melody might linger on when all else is forgotten.

Composer and Musicians

It would be difficult to think of the best animated features without the music that went with them. Even well-known shorts have signature tunes that immediately identify them. The advertising jingle is in itself a complete musical form that is closely related to the animated commercial in summing up the feeling of a product in a few seconds.

Ideally the music should blend in well with the animation that it is hardly noticed, but this rarely happens. Only too often, the music is added after the film is made, and contributes little more than the piano accompaniment to a silent film — taking its mood from the film incidentally, rather than being integrated with it. Conversely, composers are sometimes given tight storyboard specifications to work to, only to find that the script has been changed (without their being notified) and the music is nine and a half bars short.

The composer should be called in at the earliest stage possible after the storyboard has been drawn up. Suggestions on pace, rhythm, instrumentation and effects should be discussed. These need not be deeply technical; the idea of using a tuba for an elephant's walk, or violins for the sound of wind, is perfectly understandable to the layman. Characters can also be identified with sounds (the harp arpeggio for the good fairy), and instruments be made to 'talk' to each other.

Discuss ideas with musicians and see how instruments can be used for effects and how unusual rhythms create a sense of unusual movements — which in themselves might suggest shapes (triangles rotate nicely to a waltz time). Listen to records of bird sounds, musique concrete, computer generated sounds, heartbeats, etc. Try to mentally put images to them. It is the total effect of sound and image that makes animation what it is.

Sound engineer

If you have a good idea what the sounds should be like *before* you go to the studio, discuss this with the engineer prior to recording, eg: you might want a hollow echo, a laugh, or footsteps. He can advise on this and offer a range of effects. If you are not sure what you want, then record a part of the track and listen to it played back with various effects until it sounds right, then continue with the recording. If the engineer knows what sounds you want, he can set up the recording to get this right away (saving time and expense) instead of having to play around with the track afterwards.

118

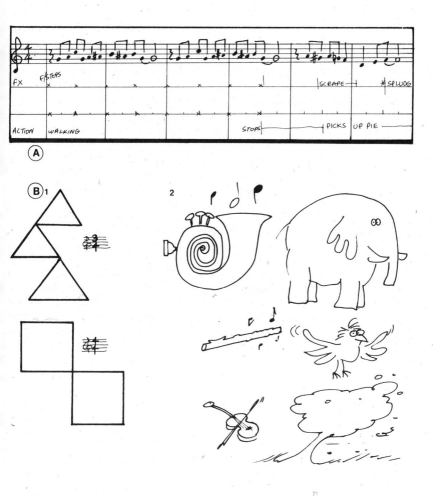

INTERPRETING THE MOOD

A. When close co-ordination between music, effects and action is required the composer would work on a chart, which like the bar sheet used by the animator, gives him all the details of timing that he needs to know. B. Musical associations. 1. Rhythm. Triangles move well to a 3/4 time (waltz tempo). Squares move well to 4/4 time. 2. Timbre. Elephants could be associated with a tuba, small birds with a flute, the wind with a violin.

AV and Film Department Man

Large companies that sponsor films regularly, often have their own audio-visual department and film library. The man in charge of this knows which films are the most popular, who uses them, and who made them. He is responsible for getting films in from other libraries, and keeping the tapes and artwork made for in-house presentations. Check with him and find out any background information about the film you are working on. See if it has been in the pipeline for long, and, if so, why. Find out who the company has worked with before, and if they still use them for film making (or have they come to you as a last resort?). Ask him to screen anything that he thinks relevant to the job you are working on, and get any leads you can.

The confidence man
Although no film industry could exist without them, the confidence man should be well down on your list of people to meet. Unfortunately the writer is the most likely person to meet him, as he exists on getting ideas for nothing and selling them at a profit.

A common technique he uses is to suggest that he knows someone who is looking for scripts and ideas, that if you have some he will present them for you and, if accepted, you will get the job. He does this with several people, also borrowing showreels and artwork on the same basis. He then approaches a producer (who may not have asked for anything!) and puts forward a proposition on the basis of your ideas. These ideas he presents as his own or, at least, presents your work as part of his package. He cannot lose because if the ideas are accepted then he takes a cut without having contributed anything and, if not, then *you* will have worked for nothing. A genuine agent would put you in touch with the others involved, and would state what he expects by way of a commission. But a con-man will continually suggest that a little more effort on your part will clinch the deal. There is no foolproof answer to this problem because con-men are clever charmers and appear generous. So:
1. Never do speculative work unless you are fully aware of who is involved and what you expect to gain.
2. Make sure *anything* you put on paper is copied, dated, named, and registered with your bank or union before handing it over.
3. Where possible, get something in writing – even receipts that can be used as evidence.
4. Never hand out material without giving a deadline on its return.
5. Check if you have the slightest suspicions.
Remember, con-men survive because they know enough about the business and people to seem plausible, so get all the information you can first.

PEOPLE YOU MEET

A. The film department man. Check on how the company uses its films and audio-visual material. B. Beware the confidence man. If you are suspicious, check around. Make sure you are included in client meetings. Make sure films, scripts or showreels that you lend out are returned by deadlines. You can safeguard your material by sending a copy in a registered envelope to your bank or union.

Markets

For most people, animated feature films sum up what animation is all about, yet they are an almost insignificant part of the total market for animation. There are several reasons for this that include the huge cost, the time (in years) to produce, the need for guaranteed distribution, the lack of large studios to handle this type of work and the scarcity of ideas to sustain an hour or so of animation. This last problem is evident in that most animated features are adaptations of books, comics, and records that are already well established in the children's markets.

Box office

People do make feature films of their own ideas, in small studios, for adult audiences, but they are usually speculative ventures and not part of the world where 'box-office' is the magic word. To be 'box-office' means competing with live action entertainment and, in turn, having a dramatic content above that normally associated with animation.

Dramatic content in some way or other means conflict. This can be seen in the popular animated features: *Snow White* against the wicked queen; *Peter Pan* against Captain Hook; *Pinocchio* against his conscience; *Dumbo* against the society that considers him a freak and outcast; *Gulliver* against the Lilliputians; *Alice* against the inhabitants of Wonderland who won't help her get back home, or accept her sanity; *Mowgli* in the Jungle book, against Sheer Khan the tiger.

Adapting such well known stories for animation requires considerable teamwork on the part of the writers, designers, composers, directors (features have several art directors) and others *prior* to the script being written, so that there is a consistency of approach. This allows the stories to retain their original feeling, yet still be cinematically acceptable.

Establishing character

For any long animated film it is first necessary to establish the characters and then build up the situations around them. Situations can be suggested to suit the capabilities of characters, and opposing characters defined who are roughly mirror-images in that they balance out the power between the goodies and baddies.

For fairy-story situations try to think of moral attitudes that sum up the situations: 'Love conquers all', 'Faith heals everything', 'Be true to yourself', and so on. These axioms are implicit in most of our fables and folklore.

Having worked the characters roughly, give them a hierarchy — or pecking order — so that their relationships are clear-cut. Avoid bringing in 'dummy' characters simply to resolve a situation; all characters must have some depth. There is no rule to creating a personality, but you might ask yourself if you would wear them on a T-shirt.

LOOK FOR THE CONFLICT

Feature films. Conflict. Peter Pan, Gulliver's Travels and Cinderella.

The Series

Producing twenty-six half hour series is comparable to making a dozen features – at least in length, but there are many differences. The Series is very much the 'production line' way of film making. The films have to be produced quickly, cheaply and, in consequence, are usually well below the standard of the feature.

These films are made for the small screen so do not use elaborate backgrounds. There is also a limit on the number of characters, and action that can take place, so most shots tend to be mid-shot to close-ups, and use much more dialogue than in other animation.

A series depends heavily on the interaction of characters rather than action and situation, and this comes down to a study of relationships within groups. For a group to hold together there has to be a contribution from each of its members. A typical group might have:

A *Leader:* the one who initiates the action, takes decisions and generally sets the style of the group; The *Leader's Buddy:* could be second in command, friend-in-need, or girlfriend; The *Brain:* the one who knows all the answers but is not the action man; The *Joker:* always has a smart line of talk and is appreciated or despised for it, as the situation demands; The *Yes-man:* goes along with everything, whether he likes it or not; The *Moaner:* disagrees with everything, but can't offer much in alternatives; The *Idiot:* does everything wrong but everyone loves him.

Peripheral characters get drawn into the group as needed, and there may be duplication of characters (contenders for leadership, etc.). Bearing in mind that we all do things in apparent contradiction to our nature, the Idiot will sometimes win out where the Brain makes silly mistakes. Also, the Good and Bad groups of opposing sides will have roughly the same type of hierarchy.

Irregular series
Typical of these would be *Mickey Mouse, Bugs Bunny, Tom and Jerry, Mr. Magoo,* etc. The characters are highly defined and identifiable. The films assume that we know them as well as we know our favourite film stars. The stories are created around their personalities. The situations are universal, and basic enough to stand viewing for years.

The characters work because they sum up a type of person perfectly, and show how their life is an extension of their personality, eg: Donald Duck gets into trouble all the time *because he is bad-tempered,* and is not bad-tempered because he gets into trouble. Bugs Bunny, on the other hand, does not get bad-tempered because he can always outsmart everyone. because the actual situations are built around their characters, it would be difficult to make a situation where Bugs Bunny met Donald Duck because no situation could be an extension of both of them.

124

STUDYING THE SERIES MARKETS

A. The TV series. Stories are usually developed around groups having the usual stereotyped characters; the Boss, the Girlfriend, the Brain, the Joker, the Idiot, the Dreamer, etc., allowing different emphasis to be placed on different characters throughout the series. B. TV demands simplicity, so close ups are used extensively, action gives way to talk and background detail is very limited. C. The cinema series is usually developed around an individual character with a strong personality.

125

Entertainment shorts

Generally speaking, a 'short' is anything under half an hour, and in animation, mostly under ten minutes. It is a single film that is, usually, a speculative production made by individuals, or studios having some spare time. 'Short shorts' are anything from a few seconds to a few minutes long. They are popular because they can sum up an idea without having to fit a time slot, so have a natural length for the idea.

In one way, the short is the ideal animation format. It can be totally made by one or two people, and done quickly enough for its authors to retain their enthusiasm all the way through (not a common asset in most animation). The big disadvantage is that it may have distribution problems. This can in some cases be overcome by putting two or more ideas together in one package.

The 'short' allows ideas to get produced that otherwise would have no outlet. So development of techniques, new applications, and new styles are tried out in shorts (studios doing features often develop ideas in shorts and later incorporate these in the features). Animation film festivals are almost totally made up of shorts, and most prize winners of the 'Best Film' category fall into this group.

Writing shorts

1. Just about any idea can be made into a short, but the best are usually humorous ideas showing aspects of human nature (as against animated jokes), and are ideal if the idea has a twist in the ending. But getting a good ending means thoroughly analysing the idea for all its possibilities. Let us take a simple idea and see how it can be treated:
The Flower: Imagine a man walking along and finding a flower; what could he do with it?
1. He might pick it and wear it as a buttonhole (vanity)
2. He might pick it and give it to someone (love)
3. He might pick it and pull off the leaves (aggression)
4. He might pick it from someone else's garden and get chased (envy)
5. He might try and pick it but find it does not yield, he then uses force and tries to destroy it (perversity)
6. He might pick it and just admire it for its beauty (culture)
7. He might try and pick it but be stopped, it then becomes a mania with him to get it (frustration)

Shorts tend to be based upon the development of simple ideas that sum up human idiosyncrasies. Take something like a car, a house, a musical instrument, that a person can use to express his or her personality and explore as many lines of thought as possible.

126

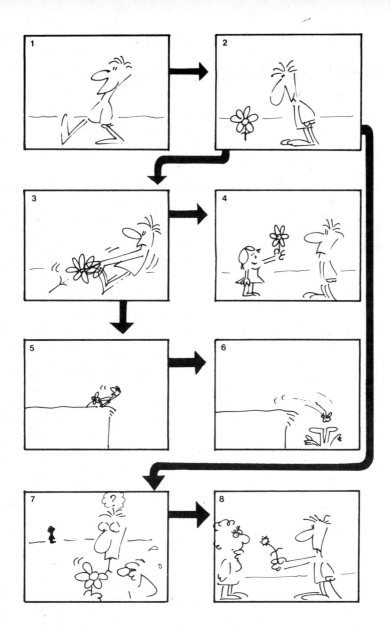

VARIATIONS ON A THEME

The entertainment short.
The flow chart method of working out variations on an idea.
1, 2, 3, 4. A man sees a flower. He tries to pick it using force but a little girl succeeds with gentleness.
1, 2, 3, 5, 6. Man fails to pick flower by increasingly forceful methods. Finally uses bomb. Blows himself up. Flower lands on his grave to grow again.
1, 2, 7, 8. Man picks flower. Wants to give girl but is shy. Pulls off petals saying 'she loves me, she loves me not'. Finally gives girl what is left of flower. Girl refuses.

Advertising Commercial

In something like thirty seconds or less, you have to say something about a product or service that is unique enough not to be confused with a similar offering, memorable enough for the viewer to recall it easily, and positive enough for them to be favourably disposed towards it. You can assume that there will be money and talent available if you have the right idea. How do you start?

Unique selling point proposition (USP)

Every product has a USP if you can find it. It may not be a particularly useful one, but it is a starting point. Every aspect of the product should be considered.

1. *Is it new?* Offering benefits not offered before?
2. *Is it old?* Offering traditional and accepted benefits?
3. *Is it cheaper than its rivals?* Making it a bargain?
4. *Is it dearer than its rivals?* For those who like the extra luxury?
5. *Is it trendy?* For the young?
6. *Is it nostalgic?* For the older?
7. *Does its shape, size, or colour have appeal?* Does function or design play a part in its appeal?
8. *Does its location, associations, or attributes distinguish it?* Is it exotic, have class connotations, or specialised use?
9. *Does its name, symbol, or context make it readily recognisable?* Would you automatically expect to see it in certain places that readily identify it?
10. *Can it be used in a humorous context?* Can it stand being made fun of?

Are there songs that might be amended to include it, or an existing personality who could be identified with it? Are there events (sport, historical, travel, etc.) that might highlight it? Are there dates, times, places that coincide with it? Are there stories, quotes, clichés, etc., that fit it?

Think of those commercials that you remember — and why you remember them. Check others with your friends. You will probably find that the design, soundtrack, and presentation were so consistent with the product you were unaware of them. If you use characters as presenters, then they have to communicate directly with the audience and not just act out an attention-getting gag. Think of the screen like a vaudeville stage where the actors are talking directly to the audience. Make sure the characters can be identified with, and that the voices are consistent and believable. And lastly, if there is a pack shot, try to incoporate this into the story, not just pop it on as an afterthought.

CREATING A MNEMONIC

A. The advertising commercial. Keep the associations with the product clear so that the animation is always consistent with the message. B. When combining animation with live action, keep the live action as stills for pack-shots or backgrounds so as not to compete for attention. C. Make shapes, colours and movements work constructively instead of just decoratively.

Teaching Films

Educational films have the advantage of a clear-cut content, context (relation to other material), and market level — which means the writer has a solid basis for a script. The disadvantages include the normally very low budget and excess of material to get into one film.

If the subject is unfamiliar, then first check for charts, diagrams, and illustrations that lend themselves to animation. See how much information these give before resorting to screen text and explanatory commentary.

Select the most self-evident pictures. Have them redesigned, coloured and composed as screen images and write a scene around the images. The images may not tie up logically at first, and there may be too much material. But the main thing is to get from excessive written book material into excessive drawn screen material.

Next, pick out the three key points of the film and edit out all material not having a direct bearing on these. Expand the key points until they tie up logically. Where the subject is not self-evident in the images (requiring text or formulae on the screen) it is better to show several examples of the subject, or sum up each stage before going on to the next one.

The common problems of teaching films appear in the early script outline stages, where treatment and approach have to be defined. As a teaching film is usually a last resort to 'get a subject across', it may have gone through several committees and had all sorts of amendments and changes since first proposed. It may then be handed over to a teacher or someone with little knowledge of film production and they will be asked to produce a fully-written script for approval before going ahead with a storyboard. In effect, this could mean producing a very literary script to satisfy the client, and quite unsuitable for visual treatment. Again, the rough sketches accompanying the script are often thought of as the final designs. As a lecturer is, in his own sphere, both writer and presenter, it takes quite an argument to convince people that a scriptwriter and actor, neither specialised in the subject, can do a better job — the expertise being translating material from one medium to another. The best way is to show films, any films, that are similar enough in style and content to indicate what the result will be like. Check the film libraries for such films.

The overriding argument is that people who watch teaching films are a captive audience. They see them because they want to learn something, and are therefore more attentive than for other films. They will only learn if the key points are made clear and memorable. If they have to reflect upon each point, are uninspired by the treatment, are talked down to or given a film version of a classroom lecture or book, then the point of having a film has been lost.

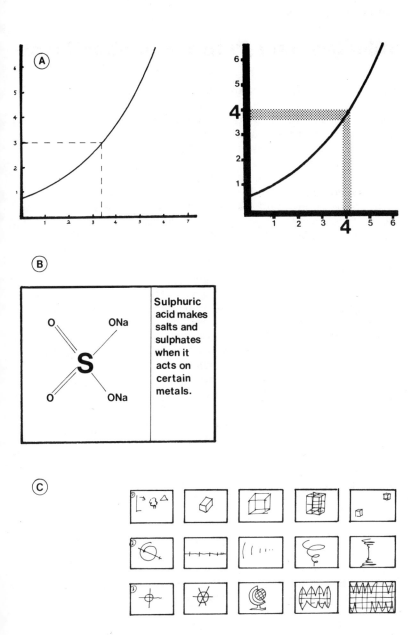

MAKE LEARNING EASY

A. Isolate information with colour and movement. B. If the text or narration is technical it can be put on a split screen alongside the animation. The text can be coloured and animated at key points. C. Prior to the final storyboard, take the key points of the subject and develop these as small storyboards. When they work, integrate them into the storyboard proper.

Industrial and Public Relations Films

Many large companies make public relations films describing the products and services they offer. Such films are not straight commercials but have a documentary and educational value. They are often freely available to the public so must have entertainment value as well. It can be quite difficult to satisfy all the demands of such a film.

Formula writing

There are a few standard themes that come up time and time again. These can be used to start with so that all the basic facts can be hung upon them, and then restated later in a more original format.

The historical approach takes the product back to the days when it first began, and even shows what people did before the product/service was available. An extreme example is the cave-man to spaceman approach. This brings out all the significant points of development and defines the essential needs that are satisfied. It is also a pointer for the future, allowing for a bit of philosophy to be tagged on the end.

The guided tour theme is also common. It could be a tour around a factory, satisfied customer's establishments, the inside of a piece of equipment, even the inside of a person if this seems appropriate. The key to this approach is to create a character who is a credible guide. He or she has to be completely identified with the situation and speak with both love and authority on the subject. An example might be of an engine driver of an old steam train talking about his train as though it were a person – the philosophy being implicit in the description.

The Laurel and Hardy twist is to have a straight man saying all the clever things and the funny man asking all the silly questions that the viewer might have asked. This approach allows difficult points to be put over in a humorous way while also ensuring that they sink in.

The talking product gives its history and background and describes its job. An example might be a drop of oil animated as a character. This approach, although pure animation, has to be treated with care otherwise it can become childish.

All of the above are typical formulas that can be used to outline a structure. Once this is achieved, then the formula should be discarded and the ideas considered on their own merit.

132

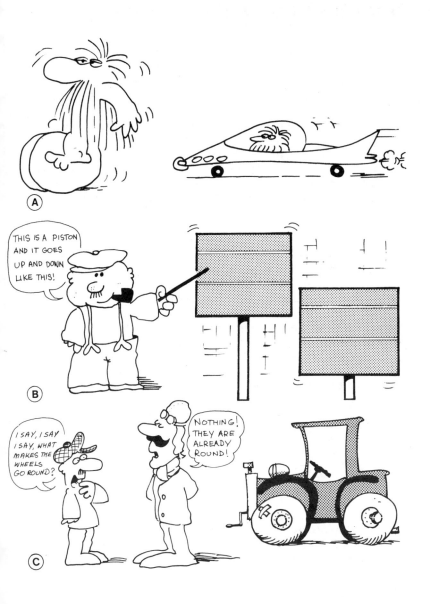

READY MADE STORY LINES

Industrial and public relations films. A. The historical approach. B. The guided tour approach. C. The vaudeville approach. Variations on the basic theme will establish the key points, then the structure can be given a more original treatment.

Title and Credits

In the late 1950s 'Film Titles' became a new area of development in animation, opening up fresh creative possibilities that could not be explored in forms of animation that needed a message.

The techniques and styles were much more dependent upon good design and camera effects than pure animation, and attracted animators to the experimental aspect of design, making much greater use of special effects.

Basic to all animated film titles is the need to set the mood and atmosphere of the live-action film. To this extent, it becomes the prologue. There are three approaches:

1. To use the live-action shots vignetted in the animated surround. This is a good method of identifying the characters with the parts they are playing. The animation becomes highly decorative, and secondary as information.

2. To animate the lettering of the titles in a way consistent with the film, eg: a horror film might have lettering dripped with blood. Here the animation will probably be superimposed over the opening shots of the live action, which will start when the titles have finished.

3. To have the titles as still text, with the animation sequence going on around them. This can be done by having a caricature of the actors in a sequence of gags and situations typical of the film to follow.

Variations on these include having the animated sequence mix directly into a matching live-action scene. Also, use 'animated links' throughout the film — which are, in effect, extensions of the titles. It is also becoming more common to create a presenter or personality using an animated character to introduce a film, although he will not actually be in it or represent anyone in it.

Not strictly animation, but often done in animation studios together with the text, is the treatment of a live-action sequence in high contrast, coloured to give a graphics effect this approach has been carried out very well in some of the *James Bond* titles, and is given heightened impact by the title music.

The music that backs the animation is important. It can lead to, or open the situations. Also characters can actively use the music, eg: dance or play an instrument. If the music has a 'period' quality, the characters might be dressed in the style of the period. Or music just to suggest effects (consistent with the film) such as when using drum beats as gunshots.

Start by writing out all the titles and credits and timing them, allowing some credits to come on singly, and others in groups. Even when used as stills, there are interesting ways of bringing on titles or credits, eg: sliding the letters on from all angles instead of just rolling down. Make sure the pace is retained all the way through, and make the end of the sequence consistent with the beginning of the film.

134

Live action vignette. Animation takes place around the live action scenes with the titles becoming decorative. Animated titles superimposed over live action background. Animated titles used as gags to set the scene. Graphic treatment of live action.

135

Experimental Films

The term 'experimental' film implies some useful exploration and development of the medium, preferably conceived within the context of the film and adding to its informational value. There are three broad areas that lend themselves to experiment:

Experiments in style
In animation, styling is the most creative way to experiment, and is virtually the basis for the development of animation. A common starting point is to take artwork from another graphics field such as fashion, illustration, photos, lithography, etc., and try to animate this style.

Advertising commercials are always looking for new styles, and it is in this field that many new designs are first applied. These designs usually come from the product, so that logos or characters identified with it are rethought in terms of movement, and are then placed in a situation built around the product. It is good practice to look at characters and styles in advertising and think of them in animation terms.

It is also useful to look at folk art where designs used for textiles, pottery, carvings, etc., suggest a field for exploration. The beauty of this field is that the characters and backgrounds are consistent with each other, and also have strong story connotations.

Experiments in technique and applications
New techniques are constantly being explored, and the benefits of these are more often to be counted in speed and cost efficiency rather than creative rewards. Typical examples might be found in cutout animation where magnetic shapes and symbols can be easily moved around on a metal board allowing simple titling benches to be used for animation. At the other end of the spectrum, computer animation can offer speed and control over technical work that might not be done as well by the animator.

The main area where techniques add to animation are not in the animation stage but in shooting and processing where optical effects can greatly enhance the existing artwork.

Animation is finding increasing applications in fields that are not strictly cinematic, ie: to be viewed by an audience for entertainment or education. Applications such as time-lapse photography for science, security, etc., sequences of X-ray pictures in medicine, or weather patterns from satellites all use animation techniques either for reconstructing images or for isolating them. It is by looking at *any* use of film which is not live-action that you will notice new areas of application — either to extend the bounds of normal animation, or to add to the existing techniques within it.

136

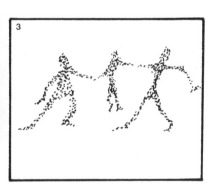

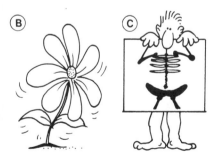

EXPLORING TECHNIQUES

A. Styles and techniques. 1. animating paint. 2. extreme simplification. 3. animating sand. 4. drawing on film. B. Time-lapse photography speeding up time. C. Animating X-ray photos.

Audio Visual (AV) Techniques

The artwork, 35mm slides, and filmstrip used for AV presentations are quite often done in the animation studio, and the work is very similar in design and subject matter to typical animation work. But there are two major differences in approach to the work. First, AV material assumes a live presenter who will be able to time and amend the presentation according to the audience response. Secondly, there is no sound track comparable to a film track.

Multi-screen AV projectors
There are many ingenious techniques in AV, using optical, mechanical, and electronic devices to simulate movement and animation. But most of these are convenient substitutes for a job that film would do better. One significant development in AV has been the multi-screen projector that uses banks of 35mm slide projectors operated automatically from a signal on a tape that may also have voice and music on it. With this, sound and image are registered.

Writing for such a system requires a good understanding of the audience level. A typical use might be at a sales conference where everyone is prepared and attentive for the message. They take the presentation as an extension of the presenter, and might expect to see familiar images, people, quotes, etc., in the presentation. The markets are highly specialised, and the presentation may only be seen once. The material should only make one point per image, so that if there is a graph showing of sales, it is better to have two pictures, one with the original and then one with the added material, so that each point is clearly established.

With multi-screens, one can put on redundant material to build up difficult and key points. Linking material can be treated more lightly, and the screens used in a decorative way, giving time for the previous information to sink in before the next key point is taken in.

Filmstrips
This is a strip of 35mm film projected from a still projector. It resembles a slide presentation but generally has a teacher winding on each frame and then talking about it for a while.

The filmstrip can be considered as a very polished version of a storyboard, but can also employ such a device as having questions for the viewer. This question-and-answer approach is very good for teaching as it allows interaction between presentation and the audience.

This medium requires a writing approach that conveys enough points for the audience to learn from it, but also allows the teacher to add further information.

138

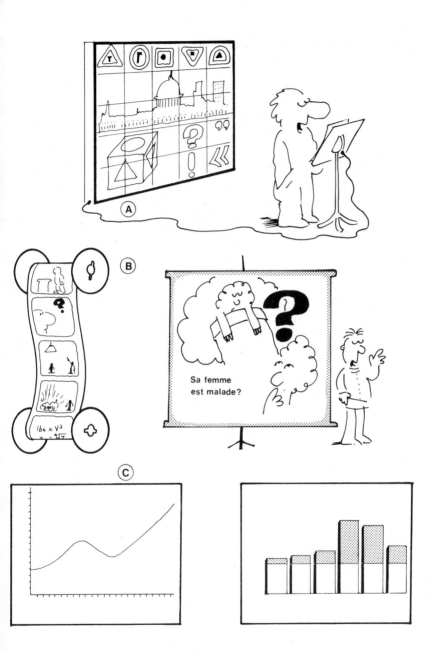

AUDIO VISUAL AIDS

A. Multi-screen projectors operated by speaker or machine. B. The film strip. The screen can contain many elements for lengthy discussion. C. Book-type diagrams are difficult to follow so make significant points into clear images.

Moving Blueprints

Computer aided design (CAD) techniques are used by engineers and architects to help them visualise situations and conditions not apparent from drawings. Typical uses would be for an architect to take three views of a building and have the computer create a 3-D model on the screen, which may then be rotated and viewed from any angle. These drawings provide the artwork for an animated film which may be shot directly from the display or from the drawings plotted on to paper. An engineer might use the system to show stress patterns building up as a piece of metal is deformed.

Although these pictures in themselves do not make a film, they can be used as inserts, or given a voicetrack, and made into short presentations. If the film is made directly on to black and white microfilm, colour may also be added. The writer may be asked to make a presentation out of such artwork.

Interactive teaching

Computer aided learning is also a growing field, and falls somewhere between films and books. It has the advantage of film in that it shows the images moving, or sequences of stills; and it has the advantage of books in that the text and pictures may be referred back to at any time.

The approach to the writing is similar to that of 'programmed learning books' where a question is posed, and a list of possible answers given. Depending upon which answer is chosen, the programme then branches to the next question. In this way the user proceeds at a speed matching his own capabilities. It is a highly specialised field, but is totally consistent with writing for animation, and this aspect of it becomes more dominant as the systems develop.

Point-of-sale gimmicks

There are many optical and mechanical effects that offer a limited animation effect. These are often seen in museums, exhibitions, and point-of-sale displays in shops. Although they do not have a story as such, they do need ideas that sum up what they represent. It is worth checking with the makers of such devices and finding out who their main clients are, also what other related devices they have. Many animated films have used such effects and, in turn, developed the related market.

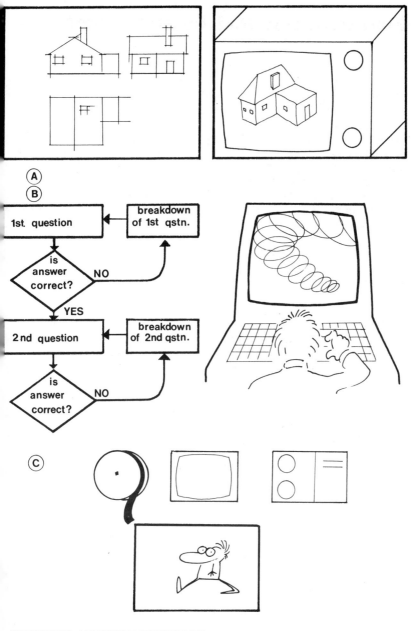

PERIPHERAL ANIMATION TECHNIQUES

A. Moving blueprints. Information on a blueprint is converted to a moving 3-D image.
B. Interactive computer programmes allow the operator to converse with the computer. C. Future developments. Film, video and computers have a common end. That of single frame control.

141

Film Festivals and Festival Films

Film festivals are market places. They are attended by film distributors, agents, programme devisers, other festival organisers, and journalists, all looking for worthy films. In their estimation a good film is one that gets good audience response.

An animation festival will have up to a hundred films in it, to be seen over a period of a few days. Considering the character of animation, this is quite a strain on the eyes. To get selected for a festival means going through a pre-selection committee who will have had to view up to five hundred entries in a week! This is, of course, a physical impossibility, and selections are usually made on seeing part of the film, so its content and message are secondary to its immediate impact and entertainment value.

The selection committee and the jury are composed of established film makers who have seen just about every type of film imaginable in animation and have a good basis for judging originality and overall competence, so will be assessing the films in terms of their contribution to the medium. The following ten points are typical reasons for rejecting films:

1. *Titles* Too long, too many, too imposing. Using puns for titles not consistent with the film. Titles suggesting that the film offers more than it does. 'Credit-overkill' with some people taking several credits when one would do.

2. *Techniques* Used badly or for their own sake, out of context, beyond their limitations or because they are fashionable.

3. *Length* The film is too long for the subject.

4. *Category.* Not properly checked by producer, so that the committee has to recategorise or reject the film.

5. *Style.* Is contrived or obviously copied; using inconsistent style, or having the styling as the sole basis for the film.

6. *Sound.* Being the sole basis for the film (animation of a record but without adding to its value) the bad use of accents and dialects in films to be seen by international audiences.

7. *Ideas.* That are unoriginal or badly transposed from another medium, imposed upon the audience, blown up beyond their value and not appropriate to animation.

8. *Status.* Of star names on the credits being assumed as a guarantee of acceptance.

9. *Ego.* Of film makers who assume that having a film is enough of a credential to submit it for a festivel. Film makers should use their own judgment on whether a film is of festival standard, otherwise they just waste everyone's time.

10. *Character of the festival.* Each festival has its own character. Check with festival lists and those with experience of the festival for the sort of films generally submitted.

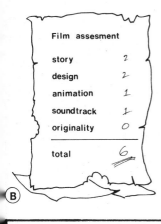

WRITING FOR FESTIVALS

A. Beware of credit overkill. A simple statement is more acceptable to selectors and viewers. B. It is common for judges to use an agreed form of assessment. C. If your film is an 'animated educational children's film' it could be eligible for one of several categories. It stands more chance of acceptance if put into a category with few entrants. Check festival catalogues for lists.

Getting Even More Ideas

Signs
If we walk down a main street or through an office block we are continually confronted with signs commanding and instructing us to Enter, Push, Press, or warning us: Danger, Private, etc. We hardly notice them, yet if they were not there, or were wrongly placed, there would be utter confusion within minutes.

Try to analyse why signs work, what they say (in effect, and not literally) and the consequences of ignoring them. Such signs can be usefully exploited in animation to convey ideas that might otherwise need dialogue. By using them in an unfamiliar way they can also be treated humorously.

Cards
Cards are available to cover almost every situation; look through a pile of Christmas cards and see how many ways there are of saying the same thing. Each attempts to sum up the spirit of Christmas while conveying something about the relationship between the sender and recipient. Take the same pile of Christmas cards and, using the theme of Christmas, see how they could be used as artwork for a story. Holiday cards can be used in the same way. The addition of drawn characters or speech bubbles can often make the card into a humorous cartoon.

Official forms
These do *not* try to present ideas in a simple direct way. 'Officialese' seems to be designed to make the simplest idea incomprehensible. On several occasions examples such as the Highway code, and Income Tax forms have been used as lyrics for songs; they can also be used as a basis for satirical films. Statements such as 'For tax purposes a married man and woman might be considered as one' lend themselves perfectly to crazy visualisation. Try designing storyboards around such forms.

Patents on inventions
A glance through a book of Victorian inventions will reveal some very odd devices. The descriptions of what these devices and machines were meant to achieve is often odder, as it reflects moral attitudes of the times as well as attempting to solve an apparently real problem. Who today would try and sell X-ray-proof corsets, or a hat that automatically raises itself to ladies? On the other hand, steam heated shoes or a bicycle for swimmers seems to embody ideas still worthy of consideration. Try to think of inventions that might be acceptable to the Victorians but seem ridiculous to us today.

SIGNS AS PROPS

Signs, whether using words or symbols, illustrate how much we rely on visual communication in our everyday life.

Getting Your Own Films Made

You may have an idea that you particularly want to do but no one wants to buy, and you can't afford to produce it yourself. There are several ways of attacking this problem, but much depends on how well you know others in the business, and how the film will be defined when it is finished.

Grants are often available from educational authorities, arts councils and various film societies. A list of these sources is available at libraries. It is important to find out how they define the conditions of sponsorship *before* submittting your idea because, if you define the purpose of your film outside of their conditions, then not only will you be turned down, but you may well find it difficult to apply again by altering your definition of the film's purpose – even if you change it.

Studios may not be open to buying your script, but might be prepared to do some work on it during a slack period. If you can persuade others in the studio to help you, it could become a co-operative within the studio. It is also possible to form a co-operative venture by advertising in the house journals of the film unions and societies.

Art schools and film schools often have students looking for projects. They may be open to looking at your work and using it as a project.

Distributors may be familiar enough with your work to guarantee its distribution *if* it is made. Given this guarantee you would be in a good position to approach a studio to take it on as a speculative venture. This would involve a deal where you get paid off if the film is distributed and covers production costs. Distributors of animated films may also be able to put you in touch with others like yourself who are prepared to discuss ideas.

Asifa is the international organisation of animation. It holds meetings, festivals, and conferences related to animation, and publishes journals covering developments and productions. The cost of joining Asifa is quite modest for which you will be kept in touch with the news in this field all over the world. It is a very good way to make contacts as it is quite common for a writer to send scripts abroad to be produced.

However you approach the problem, there is one key fact to bear in mind and that is to have a presentable storyboard fully prepared to go. It is usually a waste of time trying to 'sell' an idea that is not worked out properly as this frightens off others who might otherwise be interested.

GETTING YOUR FILM SPONSORED

The rationale

The subject is a man trying to commit suicide.

He is obviously a failure in life, and this is reflected in his suicide attempts, which also fail.

The idea of the film is that he should progressively attempt better ways of committing suicide but fail on each attempt. It is only when he decides to live that he succeeds in killing himself – making this his final failure.

The original list of possibilities included: Shooting, stabbing, poisoning, gassing, hanging, drowning, electrocution, starving, suffocating, jumping out of a window, getting run over, getting crushed, getting blown up. Disease and radiation were considered.

Taking each in turn and looking for the results of failure, the idea of a bandage for hanging himself suggested the punch line. This in turn eliminated all the possibilities that did not require a bandage such as drowning, starving, gassing, etc.

Given the bandage theme, it was necessary to have him hurt himself selectively so that he gradually gets covered in bandages. This theme dictated the order of the sequences.

Jumping out of a window meant looking for things his bandage could get caught on or in. These could be the window itself, a flag pole, balcony, protruding decorations, etc. He also had to be saved when he landed. This could be by people underneath, passing vehicles, or a shop awning.

He had to land safely and realise that life is worth living. This moment of realisation is the key sequence. It has to sum up what we all feel when we have survived a frightening situation.

He could get knocked down by a passing car, but the idea of an open manhole follows through on the drop, and is also consistent with his own unawareness.

The suggestions for music and effects were to give it a ricky-ticky sound, gaining speed as the ideas established themselves more quickly. The effects were related to the devices and colour was used sparingly for visual effects rather than decoration.

The eventual film lasted three and a half minutes – a typical length for this type of entertainment short.

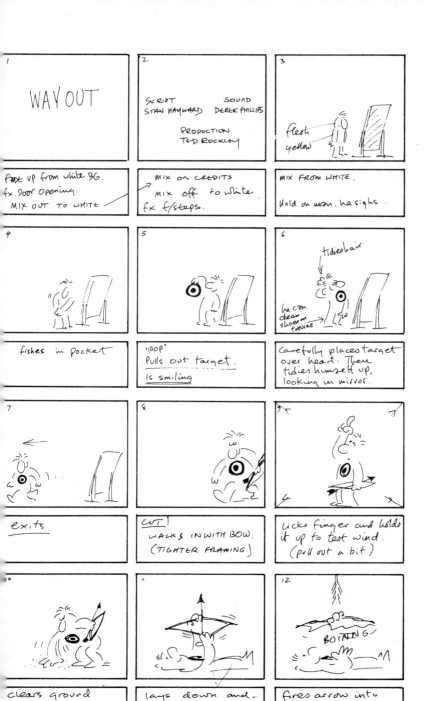

1

WAY OUT

FADE UP from white BG.
fx. Door opening.
MIX OUT TO WHITE

2

SCRIPT   SOUND
STAN HAYWARD   DEREK PHILLIPS

PRODUCTION
TED ROCKLEY

MIX ON CREDITS
MIX off to white
fx f/steps.

3

flesh
yellow

MIX FROM WHITE.
Hold on man. he sighs.

4

fishes in pocket

5

'POOP'
Pulls out target.
Is smiling

6

tidies hair

he can
dream
shoes m
trousers

Carefully places target
over heart. Then
tidies himself up,
looking in mirror.

7

exits

8

CUT
WALKS IN WITH BOW.
(TIGHTER FRAMING)

9

Licks finger and holds
it up to test wind.
(pull out a bit)

10

clears ground

11

lays down and..

12

BOING

fires arrow into
the air......
fx BOINNNG.

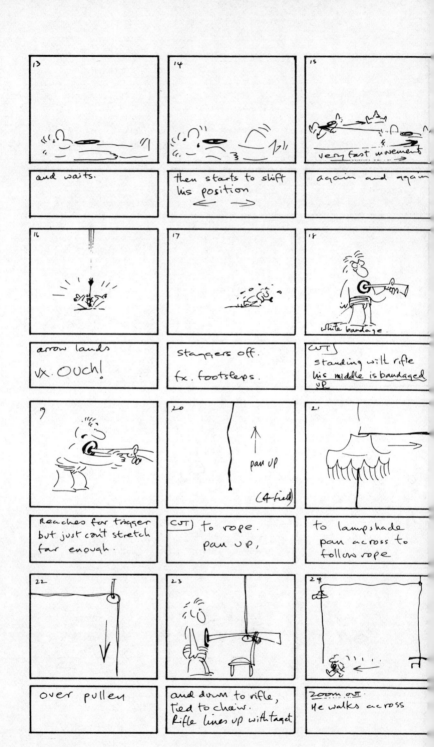

13	14	15
and waits.	then starts to shift his position	again and again
16	17	18
arrow lands vx. OUCH!	Staggers off. fx. footsteps.	(CUT) standing with rifle his middle is bandaged up.
19	20	21
Reaches for trigger but just can't stretch far enough.	(CUT) to rope. pan up,	to lampshade pan across to follow rope
22	23	24
over pulley	and down to rifle, tied to chair. Rifle lines up with target	zoom out. He walks across

Gets ready to pull rope, then suddenly gets another idea ———

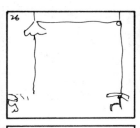

exits

Returns with ladder.

Climbs ladder and starts tieing rope into a...

noose!

puts noose around neck.

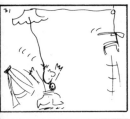

AND JUMPS.
THE LADDER FALLS OVER,
THE GUN DOESN'T GO OFF
BUT RISES IN THE AIR!

GUN CONTINUES SWINGING.
HE RESIGNEDLY PULLS THE ROPE

explosion.

Fx BANG

lampshade has fallen on him, the chairs and GUN is a wreck.

(CUT) WALKS ON WITH A PISTOL.
HIS HEAD IS BANDAGED

PUTS PISTOL TO TARGET, THEN HAS AN IDEA.

37 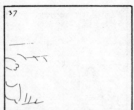 exits.	38  Returns with pistol AND Bottle of poison	39  Then has another idea
40  exits	41  Pushes on a large barrel of gunpowder	42  Lights fuse.
43  Climbs on barrel.	44  Sniffs poison, Sniff Sniff.	45  TRIES GUN. IT GOES CLICK TRIES AGAIN. STILL NO GOOD
46  Throws down gun in disgust!	47  It GOES Off and shoots him in the foot. ARRRGGGHHH!!	48  POISON BOTTLE FALLS, BREAKS AND PUTS OUT THE FUSE.

152

49

CUT | C.U. PLUGS

ZOOM OUT AND PAN →

50

PAST VARIOUS ELECTRICAL
MACHINES TO
AN ELECTRIC CHAIR
(HOME MADE)

51

don't
forget
limp.

SITS ON CHAIR, PUTS
COLLANDER ON HEAD

FOOT IN PLASTER

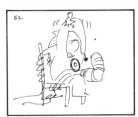

52

UNSCREWS LIGHT BULB,
THROWS IT AWAY.

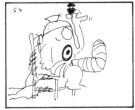

53

AND PLUGS IN

54

LOOKS SURPRISED!

FX. RADIOS, DRILLS, RECORDS
BUZZ, MUSIC. CHAOS.

55

PAN

ALL THE MACHINES ARE
SWITCHED ON

FX BUZZ, RATTLE SHAKE

56

KICKS CHAIR TO TRY
AND STOP EVERYTHING.

57

WHICH IT DOES.
HE LEANS ON CHAIR TO
CONTEMPLATE HIS NEXT MOVE.

58

ZAP!!
o o

59

CUT | A WINDOW ON A
BUILDING. THE PLASTER-CAST
LEG POKES THROUGH WINDOW,

60

EVENTUALLY HE CLIMBS OUT.
COMPLETELY BANDAGED
WITH CRUTCH.

AS WINDOW CLOSES IT
TRAPS A LOOSE BANDAGE.
HE THROWS AWAY CRUTCH

THE TRAPPED BANDAGE
TRIPS HIM UP AND
HE FALLS

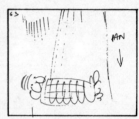

WE PAN DOWN WITH HIM,
HE UNWINDS LIKE A
COTTON REEL

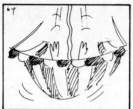

AND LANDS IN A SHOP
BLIND, WHICH BOUNCES
HIM UP AND LANDS

HIM ON THE GROUND.
HIS BANDAGE HAS UNWOUND SO
CRASH! WE SEE THE TARGET
AGAIN.

Confused he realises
that life is worth living
after all.

He tears off the target
and throws it away.

NOTICES BANDAGE.
TUGS IT TO SEE WHAT
IT IS

TAKES ONE STEP BACKWARD

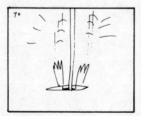

AND FALLS DOWN
MANHOLE

CRACK!!

CRACK OF NECK
BREAKING

MIX TO

END

© NGW FIELDS ANIMATION 1976

END TITLE
MIX OFF TITLE
FADE TO BLACK

154

Further Reading

ROY MADSEN:
Animated Film (1969) Interland Publishing Inc.
PRESTON BLAIR: Animation (1949) Walter Foster, New York.
RALPH STEVENSON: Animation in the Cinema (1967) Zwemmer, London; Barnes, New York.
ZORAN PERISIC: The Animation Stand (1976) Focal Press, London; Hastings House, New York.
R. FIELD: The Art of Walt Disney Macmillan-Collins, New York; London; Glasgow 1942/7
JOHN HALAS, ROGER MANVELL: Art in Movement (1970) Hastings House, New York; Focal Press, London.
JOHN HALAS: (ed) Computer Animation (1974) Focal Press, London; Hastings House, New York.
JOHN HALAS, ROGER MANVELL: Design in Motion (1960) Studio, London.
BOB GODFREY, ANNA JACKSON: The Do it Yourself Film Animation Book (1974) BBC Publications, London.
WALTER HERDEG, JOHN HALAS: Film & TV Graphics (1967) Graphis, Zurich.
BRUNO EDERA: Full Length Animated Feature Films (1977) Focal Press, London; Hastings House, New York.
JOHN HALAS, ROGER MANVELL: The Technique of Film Animation (4th ed 1976) Focal Press, London; Hastings House, New York.
JOHN HALAS: (ed) Visual Scripting (1976) Focal Press, London; Hastings House, New York.

ASIFA stands for:
International Animated Film Association (actually, *AS*sociation *I*nternationale du *F*ilm D'*A*nimation)

The address for any country can be obtained from:

ASIFA Secretariat
1021 Budapest
Voroshadsereg u.64
Hungary

Glossary

Animation Stand (Rostrum) (90) The table and camera support on which the animation is shot.

Bar Sheet (119) A breakdown of the soundtrack into frame numbers.

Cel (104) Short for cellulose acetate sheet, the transparent sheet that animators draw on.

Character (74) Animated personalities (as opposed to objects).

Dope Sheet (Camera or Exposure Sheet) (90) The animator's worksheet. It contains the track breakdown (as on the bar sheet) and matches the drawings against these. This information is then passed on to the cameraman with camera instructions.

Close Up (70) A small area of the image enlarged to the full size of the screen.

Computer Animation (97) Images generated by computer either on a screen (soft copy) or on to microfilm, paper or cel (hard copy).

Dissolve (Mix) (66) Fading out on one image while fading in on another so that there is always an image on the screen.

Double Exposure (64) The film is shot twice to superimpose two images that cannot be shot together.

Dubbing (86) The matching and recording of sound with image or sound with sound prior to the final processing.

Ease In/Out (Fair In/Out, Cushion) Terms used for the speeding and slowing down of movements at their beginning and end.

Editing (108) Broad term covering the work involved in selecting, matching, and cutting together images and sound that will be in the final version of the film.

Effects, Special (106) For animation this is usually effects added to live action to create images that could not otherwise be done.

Effects, Sound (80) Real or created sounds added to the film after it has been shot. These are usually exaggerated for dramatic effect.

Extremes (Key Drawings) The first and last drawings of a movement. These are filled in (interpolated) by an in-betweener to give the right length to the movement.

Fade In/Out (108) To go from a blank screen to the image, or from the image to a blank screen to indicate the beginning or end of a scene.

Feature Film (122) In animation anything longer than half an hour might be included in this category, but more generally refers to films lasting for over an hour.

Flip (66) The image revolves around an axis to take one scene off and bring another one on.

Frame A single picture of the film.

Freeze Frame To hold on a particular frame and stop all movement. Usually refers to a frame that has a dramatic movement in it rather than a normal HOLD.

Ghosting Giving an image only partial exposure so that it appears translucent on the screen.

Limited Animation (58) Where only part of the drawing is animated, such as the face, while the body remains static.

Line Test (Pencil Test) (89) A test shot of the animation using the animator's pencil drawings to check movement and timing.

Lip Synchronisation (Lip Sync) (86) The matching of the voice track to correctly animated lip shapes.

Logo (128) A company trade mark or symbol, commonly used for the subject of animation.

Mix (See Dissolve) (66)

Model Sheet (104) The designer's instructions on shape, proportion, colour, and size of animated characters.

Negative Image (97) A reversal of the shades or colours of the film to produce a special effect.

Object Animation (106) Using objects such as furniture, household objects, etc., for animation.

Opticals (Optical Effects). (64, 66) Obtained by reshooting the film but interposing masks, filters, etc. or adding transitions, superimpositions, etc.

Pinboard Animation Using a screen shaped-board tightly packed with pins that may be moved in and out of the board to give the effect of half-tone images when lighted.

Pop On/Off (66) The sudden appearance or disappearance of an image within the existing scene, eg: Arrow pops on to indicate a point, then pops off again.

Production Can refer to the actual film in hand, or to the total work involved in making the film.

Puppet Animation (58) 3D Articulated figures, usually hinged or wired, and used in model animation.

Rotoscoping (60) Tracing off images projected down on to paper.

Script The written plan and dialogue of the film without the visuals.

Shot (70) 'A shot of a car' refers to a single frame of the film, but 'the shot of the car moving away' refers to the short scene covering this.

Skip-Frame Usually refers to taking out every other frame to speed up the scene. Done by reshooting the film again in an optical printer or rostrum camera.

Slides Single frames used in a slide projector. Most often 35mm, but could also refer to other sizes

Squash, Stretch, and Drag Animation effects used to accentuate movements.

Stop Motion Another term for single frame shooting.

Storyboard (10, 108, 147) The visualised plan of the film containing all the necessary information for the film to go into production.

Superimpose see **Double Exposure.**

Synopsis (10) A brief outline of the film stating its objectives, concepts, and suggested treatment.

Treatment (10) A detailed description of the film covering its structure, action, and style. It may be accompanied by visuals.

Wipe (66) A scene transition using a hard edge that, in effect, wipes one scene off while bringing on another.

Zoom (Track) (70) The real or apparent movement towards or away from the artwork.